GCSE HISTORY

SCHOOLS HISTORY PROJECT

Complete Revision Guide

Allan Todd

Published by BBC Active, an imprint of Educational Publishers LLP, part of the Pearson Education Group
Edinburgh Gate, Harlow, Essex CN20 2JE, England

© Allan Todd/BBC Worldwide Ltd 2002

BBC logo © BBC 1996. BBC and BBC Active are trademarks of the British Broadcasting Corporation

ISBN: 978-1-4066-1375-9

Designed and illustrated by Oxford Designers & Illustrators

Printed in Great Britain by Ashford Colour Press Ltd

The Publisher's policy is to use paper manufactured from sustainable forests.

First published 2002
This edition 2007

Contents

About Bitesize

GCSE Bitesize is a revision service designed to help you achieve success at GCSE. There are books, television programmes and a website, each of which provides a separate resource designed to help you get the best results.

TV programmes are available on video through your school, or you can find out transmission times by calling 08700 100 222.

The website can be found at
http://www.bbc.co.uk/schools/gcsebitesize/

About this book

This book is your all-in-one revision companion for GCSE.
It gives you the three things you need for successful revision:

1 Every topic clearly organised and clearly explained.
2 The most important facts and ideas highlighted for quick checking: in each topic and in the extra sections at the end of this book.
3 All the practice you need: in the 'check' questions in the margins, in the practice sections at the end of each topic, and in the exam questions section at the end of this book.

Each topic is organised in the same way:

■ **The bare bones** – a summary of the main points, an introduction to the topic, and a good way to check what you know.

■ **Key facts** highlighted throughout.

■ **Check questions** in the margin – have you understood this bit?

■ **Remember tips** in the margin – extra advice on this section of the topic.

■ **Exam tips** in red – specific things to bear in mind for the exam.

■ **Practice questions** at the end of each topic – a range of questions to check your understanding.

The extra sections at the back of this book will help you check your progress and be confident that you know your stuff.

Exam questions and model answers

■ A selection of exam questions with the model answers explained to help you get full marks.

About this book *continued*

Topic checker

■ Quick questions in all topic areas.

■ As you revise a set of topics, see if you can answer these questions – put ticks or crosses next to them.

■ The next time you revise those topics, try the questions again.

■ Do this until you've got a column of ticks.

Complete the facts

■ Another resource for you to use as you revise: fill in the gaps to complete the facts.

■ Answers are at the end of the section.

Last minute learner

■ The most important facts in just eight pages.

How to use this book

This book is divided into three sections, sub-divided into units, which cover the three key GCSE topics of the Schools History Project specification. If you have any doubts about which topics you need to cover, ask your teacher.

For many of the units, there are corresponding sections on the video. In such cases, it's a good idea to watch the video sequence(s) *after* reading the relevant pages, but *before* you try to work through or answer the practice questions. This is because the video sequences give you extra information and tips on how to answer exam questions. It's also a good idea to write the time-codes from the video on the relevant page(s) of the book – this will help you find the video sequences quickly, as you go over units again.

The most important and popular sections of the GCSE Schools History Project specification (regardless of exam board) are covered by the book – but BITESIZE History doesn't aim to give total coverage of all topics. So it's important to carry on using your school textbook and your own notes. Because all the main types of GCSE History questions you will be tested on in the exam are covered, the general tips and suggestions will be useful, even if some of your specific topics do not appear in the BITESIZE History book. Remember, the skills are transferable to the content of any topic. Taken together, the book and the video cover all the main skills and contain all the core knowledge required in GCSE History. NB If you are studying 'Germany' as your Depth Study, you will need to view 'Germany 1919–1945' from the Modern World History unit of programmes.

How to revise for GCSE History

Instead of rewriting your notes several times over, or simply re-reading your textbook, use a variety of revision methods:

- **highlight** or underline key terms and facts in your notes
- write these key points briefly on to **index cards**
- draw **spider diagrams**
- listen to **tape recordings** of you (or a friend or parent) reading out the main points
- ask someone to **test you** on a topic
- make **visual displays** of the main points of a unit on A4 or A3 paper.

It's as important to practise answering the different types of questions as it is to learn the facts. For one History revision session, you could read through part of a topic, watch the video sequence (if there is one), and then work through the practice questions. In your next session you could read through the second part of the topic, watch any video sequence, and then do the exam question, following any exam tips given.

In particular, make sure that you look at and work through the full variety of questions, which range from:

- **short-answer source comprehension/understanding and inference/recall questions** – which simply ask you to pick out bits of information from a source and make inferences from your own knowledge about what the source does not show/explain
- **short-answer comprehension in context questions** – which require you to add facts from your own knowledge to the information given by a source
- **source usefulness/source reliability questions** – which require you to talk about a source and its provenance/origin details. Remember, even a biased or unreliable source can be useful, for example as evidence of how people thought, or as an example of propaganda
- **source comparison/cross-referencing questions** – which require you to pick out information from two or more sources and show how one source agrees and disagrees with another. Both sources will have differences as well as similarities
- **change and/or continuity questions** – which require you to analyse the extent of change or continuity from one period to another. Alternatively, you may be asked to explain why change or continuity took, or did not take, place
- **cause and consequence questions** – which ask you to describe and explain the nature of a change and its consequences
- **analysis and judgement questions** – which require you to think about the relative importance of some developments or individuals and to make a judgement (about which factor/individual was more/less important). Sometimes, you may be invited to agree/disagree with a statement made by the Principal Examiner
- **extended writing questions** – either one or two paragraph questions, or essay questions, which require you to structure the facts you have revised into a logical, planned piece of writing. This is especially important for essays. For 'why' type essay questions, in particular, make sure you don't just write down everything you know. Instead, select and use only the facts relevant to the question. Always try to do a concluding/summary paragraph.

On the day

Make sure you know which sections you have been prepared for. If in doubt, ask before the exam has started! Note carefully the total time available, and plan the amount of time you'll spend on each question, giving more time to those questions carrying the highest marks.

If there is a choice of questions, read through each one carefully, to ensure you choose the one(s) you know most about. For an essay question, make a rough plan first – it will help you find out right at the beginning whether you know enough about the topic (if you don't, it gives you time to select another). It also gives you something to jot down in the last few minutes should you get into serious time trouble – you will get some marks for a note-style answer.

Finally, don't panic! If you have followed your teacher's advice and the suggestions in this book, you will be well-prepared for any question the Principal Examiner can think up. And remember, the exam is not meant to catch you out: it is designed to help you show what you know, understand and can do.

Now read on...

Acknowledgements

AKG, London, p. 89; Ann Ronan at Image Select, pp. 45 and 102; Bildarchiv Preussischer Kulturbesitz, Berlin, p. 77; Edinburgh University Library, Shelfmark E.U.L.Or.Ms. 161, fol. 16r, p. 21; Getty Images/Hulton Archive, p.91; Mary Evans Picture Library/George Catlin, p. 9 (right); Peter Newark's Western Americana, p. 65; Science Museum/Science and Society Picture Library, p. 9 (left); The Ancient Art and Architecture Collection, p. 13; The Southwest Museum, Los Angeles, p. 98; Topham Picturepoint, p. 83; Wellcome Institute Library, London, pp. 19, 43 and 92.

Prehistoric medicine

THE BARE BONES

➤ It is difficult to be certain about prehistoric medicine because prehistoric people had no written language. Therefore, historians have to rely on deductions from archaeology and anthropology.

➤ The evidence suggests that prehistoric people had a simple dual approach, combining supernatural beliefs and natural methods.

A Supernatural beliefs

KEY FACT

1 Prehistoric people were <u>nomadic hunter-gatherers</u>, living in small groups. Life was simple, and life expectancy was low. <u>Belief in spirits</u> helped explain the many natural phenomena they did not understand.

Remember
Trephining could help relieve the symptoms of certain medical conditions, such as pressure resulting from a head injury, or epilepsy.

- Prehistoric people had little understanding of the causes of, and therefore cures for, illness.

- So magic, religion and a belief in evil spirits played an important part in prehistoric medicine. Prehistoric people consulted shamans or medicine men (witch doctors) who tried to achieve 'cures'.

- Shamans conducted rituals involving magic and charms either to cure or ward off illness. This was a form of faith or spiritual healing.

KEY FACT

2 The most dramatic way in which belief in spirits influenced prehistoric medicine was related to the belief that people could be <u>possessed by evil spirits</u>.

- The 'cure' for this was what is known as trephining (or trepanning) – drilling or cutting a hole in the skull to allow the evil spirit to escape.

Q What was trephining?

- Although trephining was (and is) a difficult operation, the evidence shows that most prehistoric people survived this procedure.

B Natural cures

KEY FACT

1 Prehistoric people also had many <u>practical or common-sense cures</u> for some illnesses and medical problems.

- The trephining of skulls actually forms a link between prehistoric supernatural and natural approaches to illness and medical treatment.

- Many skulls found from this period (some containing several holes) show that the bone had continued to grow afterwards, proving that patients recovered.

- The fact that they could successfully conduct such operations shows that prehistoric shamans possessed a fair amount of practical skill.

MEDICINE THROUGH TIME

B

2 There were also many practical and natural cures, based on <u>herbs, mosses, barks and animal fats and skins</u>.

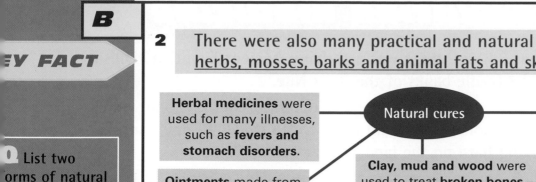

Herbal medicines were used for many illnesses, such as **fevers and stomach disorders**.

Ointments made from mosses, leaves, barks and animal fats were used for **cuts**.

Natural cures

Clay, mud and wood were used to treat **broken bones** – the evidence shows people who suffered such injuries often survived.

Massage with various substances such as saliva, sweat, or animal and vegetable fats was used– although linked to belief in evil spirits, massage helps in certain illnesses by **stimulating blood circulation**.

C Evidence

Because there is no written evidence from prehistoric times, historians rely on archaeology and evidence from more recent times.

Archaeology
Bones show that many prehistoric people survived disease, injury and even the trephining of skulls. Many **cave paintings** show various **magic and religious rituals** – some connected to hunting, but others probably attempts at medical cures. However, the absence of written evidence means that historians can only have **theories** about prehistoric **beliefs**.

More recent evidence
To help overcome this problem, historians have also examined the medical beliefs and practices of various groups who, **in recent history**, lived like prehistoric people – i.e. nomadic hunter-gatherers who had little or no contact with Europeans. Such methods are known as **ethno-archaeology** and **anthropology**. The most studied groups have been late nineteenth-century/early twentieth-century **Native Americans, Australian Aborigines and Trobriand Islanders**. By studying their beliefs, historians have tried to interpret prehistoric medical evidence such as bones and cave paintings.

Study Sources A and B, which relate to evidence about medicine in prehistoric times, and then answer the question which follows.

Source A A prehistoric trephined skull.

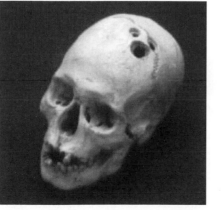

Source B A drawing of a Native American medicine man, 1830.

What can you learn from Sources A and B about medicine in prehistoric times?

MEDICINE THROUGH TIME

Ancient Egyptian medicine

THE BARE BONES

➤ By about 3400BC, there was a thriving Ancient Egyptian civilisation along the fertile banks of the River Nile.

➤ This allowed farming and the production of surplus food, which meant that some people did not have to spend all day hunting or working hard on the land.

➤ Although Ancient Egyptians invented writing, they had a dual approach to illness and medicine similar to that of prehistoric people.

A Ancient Egyptian theories and cures

1 Although the civilisation of Ancient Egypt had thinkers, priests and doctors, and was more advanced than that of prehistoric groups, there were some <u>similarities of beliefs</u> about illness – including supernatural explanations.

- Ancient Egyptians believed there were **many gods, goddesses and evil spirits**. As most illnesses had no obvious causes, they believed that **some of these gods or spirits caused or cured illness**.

- **Sekhmet** was a goddess who caused and cured epidemics; **Thoth** was the god who gave doctors the skill to cure; **Tawaret** could ensure safe pregnancy and childbirth.

- To keep away evil spirits and illnesses sent by the gods, many people wore charms – for example, scarab beetle brooches or amulets.

- Doctors often used a wide range of **prayers and spells** to 'cure' people.

2 However, like prehistoric people, Ancient Egyptians also had a wide range of natural cures, especially for illnesses with more obvious causes.

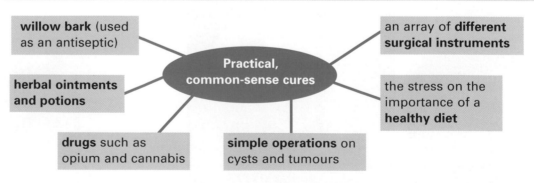

- However, even when natural cures were used, **religious beliefs** meant doctors also used **prayers and spells**.

KEY FACT

Remember
Expertise in irrigation led Egyptians to the theory of channels – some illness was said to be caused by blockages. Cures included vomiting and cutting veins.

KEY FACT

Q Name two of the Ancient Egyptian gods and goddesses associated with illness.

MEDICINE THROUGH TIME

B The influence of Ancient Egyptian medicine

1 One of the reasons Ancient Egyptian doctors influenced medicine in later times was due to <u>the invention of writing hieroglyphics</u>. These were drawn on <u>papyrus</u> (a kind of paper made from reeds).

- This allowed symptoms, treatments and the success or failure of cures to be **observed and recorded**. This, in turn, led to continuity and the **development of medical knowledge**.

- As a result, the Ancient Egyptians were able to **train doctors**, who then had to follow **strict rules and procedures**. Such doctors included **Sekhet' eanach** and **Imhotep**, who was later 'created' as a god of healing.

- Although the *Books of Thoth*, which contained all the accepted treatments and cures, have not survived, many of these spells and potions were also recorded in the *Papyrus Ebers*, the *Papyrus Edwin Smith* and the *Papyrus Berlin*.

- **This allowed knowledge and discoveries to spread** not just in Egypt, but to **other parts of the ancient world**.

2 Although the influence of Ancient Egyptian <u>religious beliefs held back medical progress at times</u> (for example, punishing doctors who departed from the cures passed down by the gods), <u>religion also helped advances</u> in medical knowledge.

- In particular, Ancient Egyptian beliefs in an after-life led to the practice of embalming dead bodies (mummification). This increased knowledge of human anatomy. (However, although embalming allowed doctors and priests to remove organs from human bodies, they were not allowed to open up those organs to see how they worked.)

- Ancient Egyptian religion **emphasised cleanliness and hygiene** – this led to such practical developments as **toilets** (although not water-fed sewers) and **mosquito nets** (which gave some protection against malaria).

- Ancient Egyptians also **bathed and changed their clothes regularly** and **shaved their heads** – these made sense given the Egyptian climate.

How did Ancient Egyptian religious beliefs both help and hinder medical progress?

Make sure that you don't just describe Ancient Egyptian beliefs – you must link them to specific examples of progress, or lack of progress, in medicine.

MEDICINE THROUGH TIME

THE BARE BONES

➤ The city states of Ancient Greece were influenced by the medical ideas of Ancient Egypt.

➤ As a result, belief in supernatural causes and cures played a big part in Ancient Greek medicine, with the cult of Asclepios being particularly important.

➤ However, at the same time, there was also a medical system based on a natural, practical approach to illness.

A Greek civilisation and beliefs

KEY FACT

1 Ancient Greece included not just the mainland and islands of Greece, but <u>many cities along the shores of the Mediterranean (Italy, Spain), the Balkans, Turkey and North Africa</u>.

• Ancient Greece began in mainland Greece in about 1000BC. By about **750BC** the cities had become **independent states**, which began to trade and then colonise areas around the Mediterranean.

• Some of these city states became very powerful. **Surplus food and increasing wealth** meant that some wealthier people had time to be dramatists, sculptors and artists.

• In particular, great emphasis was placed on mathematics, science and philosophy – **thinking and debate were very important.**

KEY FACT

2 Like the Ancient Egyptians, <u>most Ancient Greeks believed the world was controlled by many different gods and goddesses</u>.

Remember
Anaximander's idea about the four elements was developed from the earlier ideas of Thales of Miletus, who had claimed that water was the basis of all life.

• However, some **philosophers** began to replace supernatural explanations of life with **new rational and natural ones**. In about **560BC**, Anaximander (born c.610BC) suggested that all things were made up of **four elements**:

Q How were medical ideas in Greece similar to those in Ancient Egypt?

• The Greeks' ideas about medicine were also **similar to, and influenced by, those in Ancient Egypt**. The poems of Homer show that doctors gave **practical, common-sense treatments** for wounds suffered by soldiers.

B The cult of Asclepios

1 Despite the more rational approach of philosophers, religious and <u>supernatural beliefs continued to be more important for most people</u>, including in medicine.

- The most famous of the cults connected to medicine was that of **Asclepios, the god of healing**. His temples were called **Asclepions**, and were used for treating the sick. Patients stayed at the temples for at least one night.

- Three of the most important Asclepions were at **Epidaurus, Pergamum and Kos**. These were all built (or re-built) by about **350**BC.

- At an Asclepion:

Patients first had a **ceremonial washing** in the sea.	They then made an **offering or sacrifice to the god**.	Later they slept in an **abaton** – a building with a roof but no walls, and so **open to the air**.	While they slept, Asclepios was meant to **come to them in a dream and cure them**.

2 Priests in the Asclepions visited the patients, and used ointments as well as performing rituals.

- Part of the ritual often involved putting snakes on the patients. **The snake was a sacred animal in the cult of Asclepios**.

- Asclepios was said to have two daughters – **Hygeia and Panacea** – who were also involved in the healing and treatment of the ill.

- The cult was at its **most popular in the fifth and fourth centuries** BC, and continued to flourish until about AD400. This idea of taking ill people to a religious site in the hope of a cure has continued to the present day.

Study Source A below, and then answer the question which follows.

Source A A carving of Asclepios treating a boy in Ancient Greece, c.350BC.

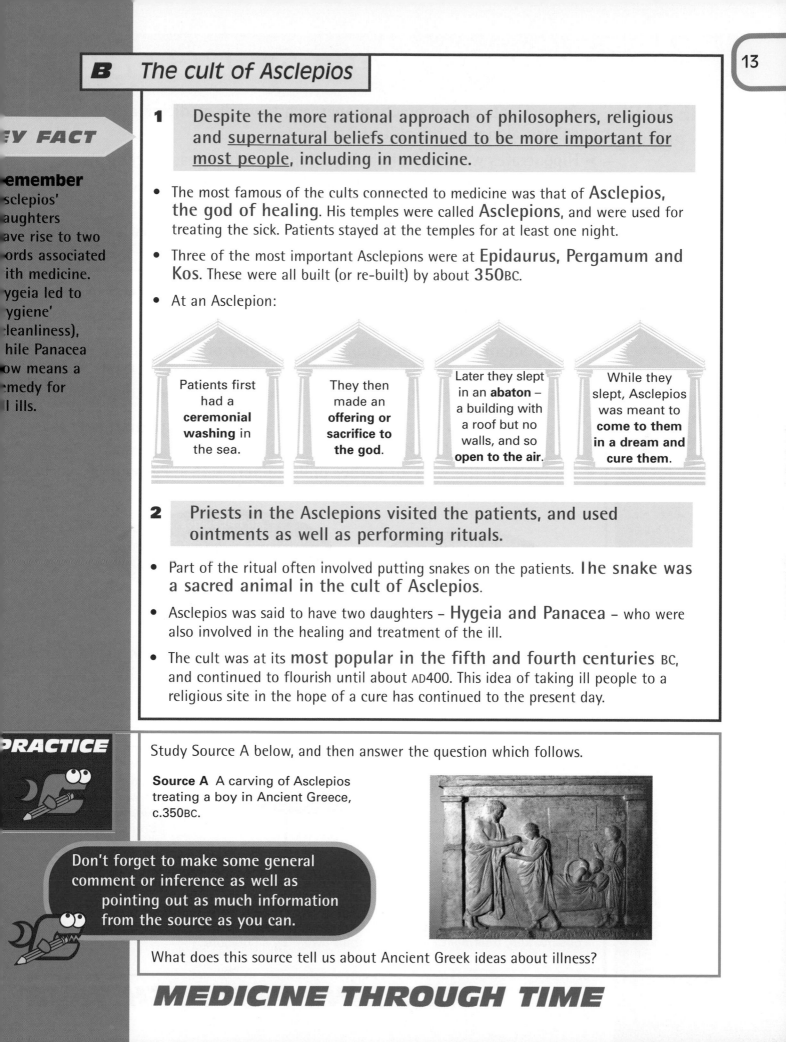

Don't forget to make some general comment or inference as well as pointing out as much information from the source as you can.

What does this source tell us about Ancient Greek ideas about illness?

MEDICINE THROUGH TIME

THE BARE BONES

➤ A more natural and practical approach towards medicine also existed alongside the cult of Asclepios.

➤ Hippocrates was particularly important, and his ideas of clinical observation were recorded and developed by his followers.

➤ Later, this led to the development of the Theory of the Four Humours, while knowledge of anatomy was advanced in Alexandria.

A   Hippocrates

1 An important <u>turning point</u> in the history of medicine resulted from the work of <u>Hippocrates</u> (c.460–377BC). He was later acknowledged as the 'founding father' of modern medicine.

- Hippocrates' approach was based on **natural rather than supernatural** explanations of illness.
- He drew on the work of earlier philosophers, such as Pythagoras (c.580–500BC) and Alcmaeon (c.500BC).

A **healthy body is one in perfect balance.**

Pythagoras

An **imbalance of hot, cold, wet or dry elements** (for example, high temperature, shivering) is **a sign of ill health**.

Alcmaeon

2 Hippocrates developed the idea of <u>clinical observation of the patient</u>, rather than just of illness itself. This was an idea also used by Ancient Egyptians.

He firmly rejected ideas about magical causes and cures, and **wanted doctors to rely on observation of patients, not religious practices**.

Hippocrates

His ideas were written down in a collection of medical books, known as the *Hippocratic Corpus*, although it is not known how much of them he wrote himself.

His ideas were developed by his followers. Clinical observation came to be based on four aspects: **diagnosis, prognosis, observation, treatment**.

His ideas also resulted in the **Hippocratic Oath**, which became a **code of conduct** for doctors and is still sworn by all doctors.

KEY FACT

Remember
Hippocrates said little about the causes of disease. His emphasis was more on studying the symptoms and course of an illness than on treatment.

KEY FACT

Remember
Hippocrates placed great emphasis on 'regimen' in maintaining good health.

Q What were the four aspects of clinical observation?

MEDICINE THROUGH TIME

B Aristotle and Alexandria

Q List the main points of the Theory of the Four Humours.

1 Hippocrates and his followers had mainly concentrated on the observation of the symptoms and course of illnesses; <u>Aristotle (384–322BC) developed their work into a theory about the causes and treatments</u> of illnesses.

- Aristotle **built on the ideas of Hippocrates**, as Hippocrates had done with the work of earlier thinkers.
- Aristotle said that the body was made up of **four liquids, or humours**:

blood	phlegm
yellow bile	black bile

- This was known as the **Theory of the Four Humours**. It was linked to theories about the four seasons and the four elements.
- Aristotle suggested that **any imbalance** – for example, too much phlegm – between these four humours was **the cause, not the symptom, of illness**.
- Treatment given by doctors was therefore based on the need to **'restore the balance'** between the humours: 'bleeding' to get rid of excess blood; vomiting if there was too much bile.
- This idea influenced the practice of medicine for **over 1500 years**.

2 Progress in medicine also resulted from the <u>founding of Alexandria</u> in Egypt by Alexander the Great in 332BC.

- Aristotle had been Alexander's tutor, so Alexander ensured that the **library in Alexandria** had a huge collection of important medical books. It soon became **famous in the ancient world**.
- **Dissection of human bodies** was allowed, as philosophers like Aristotle said a person's soul left the body after death. For a time, even the **vivisection of living criminals** who had been sentenced to death was allowed.
- The emphasis was on **accurate observation**. This enabled **progress in the study of human anatomy**, such as the discovery of the movement of blood around the veins.

3 The <u>legacy left by Ancient Greece</u> was important. Alexandria became famous for its study of surgery and medicine.

- **Doctors who had trained in Alexandria practised all over the Mediterranean world**, spreading Greek ideas about medicine.

1 Which philosopher developed the Theory of the Four Humours from the ideas of Hippocrates?

2 Why was Alexandria important for the development of medicine?

MEDICINE THROUGH TIME

Roman medicine (1)

THE BARE BONES

➤ When the Romans conquered the Greek states, they adopted many Roman ideas, including ones about medicine.

➤ Like the other civilisations of the ancient world, and as in prehistoric times, the Romans believed in supernatural causes and cures.

➤ However, the Romans also had a very practical approach to certain public health issues.

A   Roman beliefs

KEY FACT

1   As the Roman empire expanded around the Mediterranean, it began to <u>conquer the city and island states of Ancient Greece</u>.

- The Romans thought their own culture was better than that of Ancient Greece, which they had taken over. So, at first, they **rejected many of the Greek ideas about medicine**.

- Greek doctors were made slaves, and their knowledge and skills were feared. As a result, **medicine in Ancient Rome had a low status**.

KEY FACT

2   However, an <u>outbreak of plague</u> in 293BC led the Romans to set up an <u>Asclepion in Rome</u>. They even brought a sacred snake from Epidaurus.

Remember
The Romans, like the Ancient Greeks, believed in a number of different gods and goddesses. However, they tended to be more interested in practical buildings than in temples and shrines to the dead.

- The Asclepion lasted throughout the Roman period, and became a **public hospital**, offering treatment to the poor and to slaves.

- Later, medicine and its mainly Greek practitioners, slowly improved in status. Then, **in 46BC**, Julius Caesar gave Greek doctors the right to become Roman citizens. As a result, **Greeks came to dominate the medical profession throughout the Roman empire**.

- In this way, the medical traditions of Ancient Greece survived, leading to **continuity in medicine in the ancient world**. However, it is important to remember that Greek ideas were often mistaken. Diocles (fourth century BC), regarded as the second greatest Greek doctor after Hippocrates, worked in Athens where human dissection was not allowed. As a result, he studied animals and **so made no progress in human anatomy**. However, he did also write about **diet and the medicinal uses of plants and herbs**.

- At first, however, there were very few doctors in Ancient Rome, so the **head of each household was supposed to treat all its members**. People used a mixture of **common-sense methods** and a range of **rituals based on traditional beliefs in the supernatural**.

Q Why was the outbreak of plague in 293BC important?

B Public health

1 The Romans were a <u>very practical</u> people, and came up with many <u>technological developments in engineering and architecture</u> to solve certain health problems.

These inventions were **based on observation.** For example, they noticed that more **people became ill** when exposed to **bad smells, unclean drinking water, swamps and dirty conditions.**

In particular, they noticed that **even if temples to gods were built in such places,** and supernatural rituals (such as sacrifices and offerings) were followed, **people still became ill.**

So they tried to overcome these problems by practical methods. This led to **progress in public health.**

2 <u>The Romans made several important developments in public health</u>, which have had influence right up to the present day.

Aqueducts were built to carry **clean drinking water** into towns and cities. There were 14 aqueducts in Rome.

Roman public health measures

Toilets, public toilets and **sewers** were built to carry the waste away. There were 150 public toilets in Rome.

Public baths were built for cleanliness.

Swamps and marshes were drained to deal with fevers. This was based on the belief that it was bad smells (not the malaria-bearing mosquito) that caused illnesses.

- As well as these public facilities, the richest Roman citizens also had their own private facilities.

- However, areas where the poor lived were not supplied with running water to houses or with lavatories connected to the sewer system.

- The poor had to use public taps and fountains, which were placed in the streets, and chamber pots were often tipped out into the streets rather than into sewers.

Q Why was he building of queducts mportant?

Q Why did the omans drain arshes and wamps?

1 Which Roman ruler, in 46BC, allowed Greek doctors to become Roman citizens, so ensuring that Greek medical knowledge and practices continued in Ancient Rome?

2 Name two technological improvements made by the Ancient Romans in the area of public health.

MEDICINE THROUGH TIME

Roman medicine (2)

THE BARE BONES

➤ The Roman empire placed great emphasis on war. This not only led to rapid expansion of the empire, but to some important developments in medical knowledge.

➤ The medical ideas of Ancient Greece continued during this period, but there were also developments associated with individuals.

➤ Galen's work was particularly important – he put together a single system of existing medical knowledge and his own discoveries.

A   War and medicine

KEY FACT

Q Why was war important in the development of medicine in Ancient Rome?

1   One area where the Romans' <u>practical approach to medicine</u> had a big impact was connected to war.

- The Roman state realised that to establish and then control a large empire, it would need a large and **healthy army**.

- So sites for military camps and bases were usually chosen to ensure **supplies of fresh and clean drinking water, and the safe disposal of sewage**.

- The government also paid to set up **hospitals for wounded soldiers**. These were called **valetudinaria**.

KEY FACT

Remember
The Romans eventually extended the system of hospitals to cover civilians as well.

2   The Romans also provided <u>special doctors</u> for soldiers.

- One of the most important of these doctors was **Dioscorides**. He was a Greek doctor, born in Turkey, who worked for the Roman army **around** AD80.

- Dioscorides was the first to record the **medical uses of plants** in his book, *De Materia Medica*, without adding lots of supernatural charms and rituals. His book was used by doctors for over **1000 years**.

- The Roman army also had **special medical troops** who treated wounded soldiers on the battlefield.

B   The importance of Galen

KEY FACT

1   <u>Galen</u> was a Greek, born in Pergamum, Turkey, in about AD129. He <u>supported the ideas of Hippocrates</u> and his followers, and also <u>increased his own knowledge of anatomy</u>.

- Galen followed **Hippocrates' ideas of observation** and believed in the **Theory of the Four Humours**. He also accepted Hippocrates' ideas about ethics. This led to **continuity in medical knowledge and practice**.

B

Remember
Deprived of human bodies, Galen dissected animals (barbary apes, pigs, dogs) instead, so he made several mistakes.

KEY FACT

Q Why did Galen make several mistakes about human anatomy?

Q Why were Galen's books important?

Galen trained as a doctor in the Asclepion at Pergamum and then at Alexandria. However, by then, human dissection had been banned for religious reasons so only skeletons could be studied.

But as a doctor to gladiators, Galen was able to increase his knowledge of human anatomy while treating their wounds.

When Galen moved to Rome, he found that even the study of skeletons was banned. However, he managed to study both the bones of criminals and bodies washed out of cemeteries during floods.

2 Galen developed many treatments based on the <u>theories of balance</u> and <u>treatment by opposites</u> although he only wrote about his successes, not his failures.

- Galen also gave lectures as well as **writing over 100 books**.

These drew together the ideas of all the great doctors of the ancient world in the 500 years since Hippocrates.

He fitted all these ideas into a single system, dealing with observation, diagnosis, treatments, surgery, anatomy and physiology.

Many of his books survived the fall of Rome, and so his reputation lasted through the Middle Ages and into the Renaissance. His work formed the basis of doctors' training for the next 1400 years.

PRACTICE

Study Sources A and B, and then answer the question which follows.

Source A An extract from a history textbook, published in 1996, about dissection in Alexandria.

> Dissection was allowed in Alexandria – for a short time even dissection of the living was carried out. Criminals who were condemned to die were dissected and consequently the movement of blood around the veins was discovered. This practice was soon stopped. But dissection of the dead was still carried out, and advances in anatomy were made. The work carried out at Alexandria stressed accurate observation of what was actually there.

Source B Galen dissecting a pig, from a 1556 edition of *Galen's Collected Works*.

Make sure you do BOTH things asked in the question – use the TWO sources AND your own knowledge.

What continuity was there in the development of medical knowledge between Ancient Greek and Ancient Roman times? Use the sources and your own knowledge to explain your answer.

MEDICINE THROUGH TIME

Islamic medicine

THE BARE BONES

➤ After the fall of Rome in the fifth century, there was a regression in medicine across Europe.

➤ But much of the medical knowledge and the books of Ancient Greece and Rome were kept alive in the East.

➤ Some important medical developments took place in the Islamic empire, and later spread to Europe via the Crusades and trade.

A From the Roman to the Islamic empire

KEY FACT

1 <u>In 395, the Roman empire was split into Western and Eastern empires</u> because of pressure from barbarian tribes (such as the Goths, Visigoths, Huns and Vandals) from the North and East.

Remember
Women doctors were allowed to practise in the Arab world at this time.

- From about 410, Ancient Rome began to fall to these tribes, and **the Western Roman empire finally collapsed in 476**. The conquering tribes burned books and libraries, including many medical texts from Ancient Greece and Rome.

- As a result, there was a **return to a more primitive approach to medicine and the causes and cures of illness** in Europe.

Remember
Like the Romans, Islamic doctors were prohibited from dissecting human corpses for religious reasons.

- However, not all was lost as **part of Roman culture (and medical knowledge) was preserved in the Eastern Roman (or Byzantine) empire**, which had its capital in Constantinople.

- In **431, Nestorius,** the Christian patriarch of Jerusalem, and his followers, were banished for heresy.

- They settled in Persia and set up a **centre of medical learning**, which **translated the writings of Hippocrates and Galen into Arabic.**

KEY FACT

2 Even more important in preserving the medical knowledge of the ancient world was the <u>new Islamic Arabic civilisation in the Middle East</u>, based on the religion founded by Muhammad (PBUH) (born c.570).

Remember
Many Arab doctors still believed that illness was caused by evil spirits.

- **By about 1000, this empire had spread** from the Middle East into parts of Southern Europe and North Africa. **Baghdad soon became the new capital of this Islamic empire**.

- **Arabists** (those following the Arabic school of medicine) followed Hippocrates' clinical observation, Aristotle's Four Humours and Galen's treatment by opposites.

Q Describe the important work done by Hunain ibn Ishaq.

- Especially important was the work of **Hunain ibn Ishaq (aka Johannitus)** who was **chief physician of Baghdad** when he died in about 873.

- He had travelled to Greece to **collect medical texts, which he then translated into Arabic** – knowledge that was temporarily lost in the West.

A

3 There were also <u>several important developments in medical knowledge by doctors in the Islamic empire</u> which, by the eighth and ninth centuries, had become a centre for learning and new ideas.

- **Islamic governments** set up **medical schools** and, **from 931**, doctors had to **pass exams and get a licence** before they could practise.
- Another important development was the **building of hospitals**. The **Qur'an** emphasised the duty **to care for the sick and to study medicine**. By 850, Baghdad had its first hospital; others were soon set up across the Muslim world.
- These Arabic ideas began to **spread to Europe** as a result of **trade** and the **Christian Crusades**.

emember

here were also dvances in ublic health – aghdad, Cairo, amascus and ordoba had iped water and ublic baths efore 1000.

B *Important individuals and developments*

emember

lso important as alchemy. rabic lchemists iscovered new ethods and echniques, such s distillation nd sublimation. hese were then sed to prepare rugs, and to evelop new nes – for xample, udanum nd camphor.

Rhazes (al-Razi), 860–925
He followed the Hippocratic methods of clinical observation and the ideas of Aristotle, and was the first to note the different symptoms of smallpox and measles. He wrote an important book: *al-Hawi* or *The Comprehensive Book*.

Ibn Sina (980–1037) *aka* **Avicenna**
His *Canon of Medicine* (a complete medical system based on Galen and his own new observations) was later translated into Latin, becoming **the main medical textbook in Europe until 1700**.

The Islamic empire – important developments

Abul Kasim (936–1013)
aka **Albucasis**
He was **the greatest Arab surgeon**, and wrote a book on surgery, containing advice on amputations, fractures, dislocations, how to sew wounds and dentistry.

Ibn an-Nafis
He made many observations during operations (the Qur'an forbade dissection) and **discovered some errors in Galen**. In **1242**, he said blood passed through the lungs, but no one else agreed, **so the old views continued**.

Study Source A below, and then answer the question which follows.

Source A An eighth-century drawing of Islamic doctors performing a Caesarean section operation.

What can you learn from this source about Islamic medicine in the Arab world in the period 750–1400?

MEDICINE THROUGH TIME

Medieval medicine

THE BARE BONES

➤ After the fall of Rome, there was a regression in medicine in Europe, and a return to a more primitive outlook.

➤ Although the Christian Church stressed supernatural explanations for illness, it also helped medicine recover in the Middle Ages by accepting the works of Hippocrates and Galen.

➤ But despite some improvements, medical knowledge in medieval Europe was often less advanced than in the Islamic world.

A   Medicine in the early Middle Ages

KEY FACT

1 <u>The fall of Rome was a turning point for medicine in Europe</u>, including Britain, as it began what is sometimes known as the Dark Ages.

- The peoples who took over the Roman empire **believed more strongly in superstition and magic** as the source of medical explanations and 'cures'.

- The **public health system and methods of the Romans collapsed**. Books and libraries were destroyed, and doctors were often killed.

- As a result, much **medical knowledge in Europe was lost**, and **new ideas could not easily spread** as trade and travel declined.

KEY FACT

2 Gradually, <u>the Christian Church re-established itself</u>, but this only strengthened belief in supernatural causes and cures of illness as the Church taught that God sent misfortunes (including disease) to punish sinners.

Remember
Until about 1200, there was little organised study or medical training for doctors in Europe.

The **Crusades and increasing trade** eventually led to the **medical knowledge of the Arabist doctors reaching Europe**. Also, some of **the writings of Hippocrates and Galen**, which had been translated in the Islamic empire into Arabic, were **translated back into Latin**.

The Church's approach led to an increase in the number of **pilgrimages** made by the sick, and **prayers** to God and numerous saints.

During the period 1000–1100, **the Church came to accept the works of Hippocrates and Galen**. One problem with this was that, for a long time, only some of their books were re-discovered so **much knowledge of anatomy remained missing**.

The influence of the Christian Church

Q How did the writings of Hippocrates and Galen eventually come back to Europe?

The Church discouraged changes to the ideas of Hippocrates and Galen, and instead taught that they were the absolute truth.

The Church was **strongly opposed to dissection**.

Despite the re-discovery of the works of Hippocrates and Galen, medieval doctors also relied on **astronomy and astrology**, as they believed the stars and planets could cause disease, and could be used to help decide on diagnosis and treatment.

MEDICINE THROUGH TIME

A

3 Because there were few trained doctors and they were very expensive, <u>ordinary people usually relied on a number of alternative healers and treatments</u>.

Local monks (who often believed in the four humours) prescribed **herbal medicines**. **Apothecaries sold drugs and medicine** and sometimes gave advice.

Alternative healers and treatments

Barber-surgeons also gave 'cures', but they had a very low status and surgery remained very risky.

Housewife-physicians and local **'wise men' or 'wise women'** used traditional cures, especially for help during pregnancy and childbirth.

B Main ideas and developments

1 However, medicine became <u>increasingly professional</u> around the end of the eleventh century, for both physicians and surgeons.

- In the tenth century, the **Law of Edgar** allowed women in England to train as doctors. But as medicine re-emerged as a **specialised and high-status profession**, it became an increasingly **male preserve**.
- **Increased contact with the Islamic world** led to more knowledge of Hippocrates and Galen, and to the **establishment of medical schools**. The first medical school was set up at **Salerno** in southern Italy.
- Later, more medical schools were set up and, by the **fourteenth century, medical departments were being set up in universities**.
- From about 1300, **the Church began to allow some public dissection** in universities and some revisions of Galen.

2 <u>New methods were put forward</u> (for example, analysis of urine), but acceptance of new ideas was very slow.

Hugh (d.1252) and Theoderic of Lucca (1205–1298) used wine to clean wounds. They reported its success as an antiseptic, but their idea did not catch on.

Important new ideas

Guy de Chauliac (c.1300–1368) – his *Chirurgia* of 1363 was the most important medieval book on surgery.

Mondino de Luzzi (c.1270–1326) aka Mundinus published his *Anatomy* in 1316. It became the main teaching text for the next 200 years.

1 How did the Christian Church help recovery in medical knowledge after the fall of Rome and the Dark Ages?

2 How did the Christian Church hold back development in medical knowledge in medieval Europe?

MEDICINE THROUGH TIME

THE BARE BONES

➤ There was both regression and continuity in public health after the fall of Rome.

➤ Although Roman public health measures and structures collapsed, some were preserved by the Christian Church.

➤ However, serious public health problems affected most people, as shown by the Black Death.

A Public health problems

KEY FACT

1 The Romans had developed piped water, public baths and toilets, and sewage systems for their towns. <u>These made it easy for people to be clean.</u>

Remember
Even where there were cesspits, they were emptied irregularly so they often overflowed. As a result, they only delayed the problems.

In the Middle Ages, there was **no government provision of public health facilities**, so cleanliness declined, especially among the poor.

Town corporations

Some corporations passed laws to limit the dumping of rubbish and sewage, but they **were difficult to enforce except in times of serious disease or epidemics**, which were common then.

The provision of such facilities was usually the responsibility of town **corporations**. These bodies were made up of the rich, who **did not think that public health was their responsibility**.

Rubbish and sewage were usually dumped in the streets or nearby rivers and streams. Some houses shared cesspits or built their privies over streams. Therefore, streams were often blocked with sewage and were **more like open sewers**.

During outbreaks of disease and epidemics, the corporations would **fund the collection and burning of rubbish**, but this was **never done on a regular basis**.

KEY FACT

2 The Church, and especially its <u>monasteries</u>, played an important role in <u>maintaining some continuity</u> with the public health measures of Ancient Rome.

Q Why did the corporations of medieval towns not take regular action to keep streets and rivers clean?

Monasteries had their own **drainage and water supply systems**. Often water was purified by being piped through settling tanks.

The Church and monasteries

The Church set up **hospitals for the sick** (such as St. Bartholomew's Hospital in London). These had effective sanitation, and concentrated on providing clean and quiet conditions. However, some of these hospitals were **only concerned with providing care**, not treatment.

Dirty water was drained off and used to clean their toilets, which were **kept in a separate building**.

Some monks were appointed to make sure the **laver** (where monks washed their hands and faces regularly) were **kept clean**, and that there were **plenty of clean towels and sheets**.

B The Black Death

1 Concern over public health issues came to a head in <u>1348, when the Black Death (bubonic plague)</u>, which had been spreading across Europe since 1346, finally <u>reached England</u>.

- The **victims of Black Death** suffered a high temperature, headache and vomiting, followed by lumps **(buboes)** in the armpit or groin. These then went black and spread all over the body.

- The Black Death was **spread by fleas carried by black rats**. These rats travelled across Europe in ships. There was also **pneumonic plague**, which was spread by sneezing.

Q How was the Black Death spread?

2 At the time, <u>people did not understand what caused the disease</u>, and they did not know how to stop its spread or cure it.

- As a result, between **one-third to a half of the population died**. The Black Death was **especially bad in towns** because they had greater problems with public health and the hazard of more people living closer together.

- There were **both supernatural and natural explanations** of the disease – for example, some people said that God had sent it as a **punishment**, others that the planets were in the **wrong conjunction**, or that it was caused by **'foul air'**. Sometimes, **groups of people**, such as the nobility or Jews, were said to be responsible.

3 However, it was <u>observed that the disease was contagious</u>. This led to steps to isolate the plague victims.

- But there were **no effective cures or treatments**, so people **relied on spiritual or magical 'cures'**, or took certain **'practical' steps**.

- More practical attempts included **strong-smelling posies** as a precaution against 'foul air', and the wearing of overall suits (often made from oil cloth). In fact, these did give some protection against the fleas.

- Ships newly arrived in harbour had to **wait for 40 days** before landing (this gave rise to the term **'quarantine'**, from the French 'quarante', their word for 40).

Remember
Some people, known as Flagellants, whipped themselves and each other, and prayed, to get God to stop punishing people with the plague.

PRACTICE

1 Which Church institutions helped keep alive some of the Roman public health developments, such as clean drinking water, toilets and hospitals?

2 What was the Black Death, which hit Europe during the years 1346–1350?

MEDICINE THROUGH TIME

Renaissance medicine (1)

THE BARE BONES

➤ The Renaissance, which was at its height from about 1450 to 1600, had a big impact on many areas of life, including medicine.

➤ The Renaissance (and the religious Reformation, which began about 1520) saw the re-discovery of many Ancient Greek texts.

➤ As the sixteenth century progressed, there were many developments in anatomy and medical treatment.

A Renaissance and Reformation

KEY FACT

1 The Renaissance is the term applied to the <u>rebirth of learning</u> from the <u>classical civilisations of ancient times</u>.

● During the Renaissance many **important works by earlier writers on medicine**, such as Hippocrates and Galen, **were recovered**.

● This led to **renewed faith** in the Theory of the Four Humours, treatment by opposites, bleeding and herbal medicines.

KEY FACT

2 But the Renaissance also saw the emergence of a <u>new, more scientific approach to the natural world</u>, based on <u>accurate observation</u>.

Remember
The perfect 'Renaissance man' was knowledgeable about science, as well as classical literature and arts.

● The **invention of printing** (which began with Johann Gutenberg in 1454) soon proved to be extremely important in the **rapid spread of new and more accurate knowledge and ideas**.

● The **works of Galen**, which came from the East in Arabic, were quickly translated into Latin and then printed.

● **Mondino de Luzzi's** *Anatomy* **of 1316**, with its accurate drawings of the human body, benefited from the **much more precise copying and illustrations** that printing allowed.

KEY FACT

3 Almost at the same time as the Renaissance, there was the <u>Reformation</u>, which <u>weakened the hold of the Roman Catholic Church on education and learning</u> as well as religion.

● This led to **increased debate**, and worked in parallel with the Renaissance's **more scientific outlook**, based on the **close observation and recording of nature**. In particular, **new theories were developed** to explain all aspects of the world, including medicine.

Q Why was printing important in the spread of medical knowledge?

● In **1527**, in Basel, **Paracelsus** (town physician and lecturer at the university) burnt some of Galen's books because he said they had been proved to be inaccurate. Paracelsus also rejected the Theory of the Four Humours, and said most of Avicenna's work was useless.

MEDICINE THROUGH TIME

A
- In **1531**, **Johannes Guinter** (Professor of Medicine at Paris), published a new, complete Latin translation of Galen's *On Anatomical Procedures*, which had been 'lost' in the West since the fall of Rome. This proved to be much more accurate than Mondino's work, which had itself been based on only part of an incomplete lesser work by Galen.

B *The importance of Vesalius*

KEY FACT

1 Progress in the knowledge of <u>human anatomy</u> was made as a result of the work of <u>Andreas Vesalius (1514–1564).</u>

Remember
The Church and many doctors refused to accept that Galen had made any errors. Vesalius took little part in the arguments and did not carry his research further.

Vesalius **did his own dissections**, and published drawings of his work – for example, *Tabulae Sex* in **1538**, in order to help his students. But many doctors were opposed to his methods.

In **1539**, his *Letter on Venesection* criticised the current method of bleeding, based on Galen's work on veins. But this **conflicted with the earlier Arabic translations** that had been followed since the Middle Ages and so was **rejected by many doctors**.

In **1543**, his seven-volumed *The Fabric of the Human Body* was published, with illustrations. In particular, Vesalius **rejected Galen's theory that blood passed from one side of the heart to the other** via the septum (this had already been refuted by Ibn an-Nafis in 1242).

The influence of Vesalius

Vesalius found **errors in Galen's anatomical work**, but at first did not reject Galen's teachings publicly.

KEY FACT

2 However, despite his discoveries, <u>Vesalius did not offer any new theories about the causes of diseases or cures</u>.

Throughout the sixteenth century, treatment continued to be based on **Hippocrates, the Four Humours and Galen**. (However, there were some important **developments in surgery** in the sixteenth century, resulting from the work of **Ambroise Paré** – see page 48).

The failure of Vesalius

Vesalius' findings had **little impact on the treatment** of illness.

There was a wide range of **alternatives to physicians** for the majority of the population – for example, **apothecaries, 'quacks', or local 'wise women'**, who used bleeding, herbal remedies and astrology.

Q Why did Vesalius' criticisms of bleeding have little impact on treatment?

PRACTICE

1 How did the Reformation help new developments in medicine during the Renaissance period?

2 Whose important book, *The Fabric of the Human Body*, published in 1543, made public his criticisms of Galen?

MEDICINE THROUGH TIME

Renaissance medicine (2)

THE BARE BONES

➤ The study and knowledge of anatomy continued to progress in the seventeenth century.

➤ Important discoveries about the heart and the circulation of blood were made, but they had little immediate impact on treatment.

➤ Some important inventions were also made during the Scientific Revolution, but they were of little practical benefit to medicine at the time.

A   Developments in physiology

KEY FACT

1   In <u>1603, Geronimo Fabricius</u>, Professor of Anatomy at Padua, published <u>*De Venarum Ostiolis*</u>, in which he identified the valves in veins. He also designed a new anatomy theatre in Padua, which gave a good view of dissections to everyone gathered.

- **William Harvey (1578–1657)** studied medicine at Padua under Fabricius in the years 1598–1602. In 1615, he began lecturing in anatomy at the Royal College of Surgeons in London.

- Harvey did **comparative studies** on animals (especially frogs) and humans. He also did live dissection (vivisection) of animals in order **to observe the heart**. He then began to apply his findings to humans.

KEY FACT

2   As a result of his observations, <u>Harvey proved that Galen was wrong</u> about the <u>circulation of the blood</u>. Building on the work of Erasistratus (c.250BC), he also identified <u>the differences between veins and arteries</u>.

- Harvey also showed how the **heart acted as a pump**, and **passed blood through the lungs** (changing its colour).

- These discoveries (published in his book *On the Motion of the Heart and Blood* in **1628**), were an important turning point for the development of anatomy.

- However, they **did not really change surgery or medical treatment in general** (for example, blood transfusions were not common, and were not really successful until the discovery of different blood groups in 1900).

- In the second half of the seventeenth century, **Thomas Sydenham** became one of the most famous doctors in London.

- He was known as the 'English Hippocrates' as he stressed the **close observation of patients and symptoms**. As a result, he was the first to discover a new disease – scarlet fever.

Remember
Sydenham's treatments were mainly to leave the patient alone and/or use common-sense cures. In 1676, his book 'Medical Observations' was published.

B Further developments in anatomy and treatment

KEY FACT

Q Name two inventions before 1750, which later helped medical knowledge and treatment.

1 The period 1650–1750 is often known as the Scientific Revolution, during which physics, in particular, became more established.

The seventeenth-century **interest in science and experimentation** continued throughout the period.

The Scientific Revolution 1650–1750

Fahrenheit and Celsius invented their **thermometers** in **1709** and **1742** respectively.

The Dutchman **Anthony van Leeuwenhoek invented the microscope** in **1693**.

Substances such as hydrogen, oxygen and nitrous oxide were **discovered**.

KEY FACT

Remember These developments had no real impact on medicine and the treatment of patients until the nineteenth century.

2 There were also several important developments and advances in knowledge in the early eighteenth century.

Hermann Boerhaave, Professor of Medicine at Leyden in the Netherlands, emphasised the close observation of patients and the keeping of accurate records. He also published a new edition of Vesalius' work.

One of his students, **Albrecht van Haller**, investigated breathing and digestion.

There were also some important **developments in surgery** made in London by **William Cheselden** and, later, by **John and William Hunter**.

Boerhaave's students practised in other parts of Europe (and America) and so spread his ideas. One of them, **Alexander Monro**, made Edinburgh University one of Europe's leading medical centres.

KEY FACT

3 However, despite these advances in knowledge, older alternative forms of treatment continued.

Most people **could not afford to go to a qualified doctor**. There were none available in many areas anyway.

Alternative forms of treatment were still used

Supernatural and magical cures were still used. Even many trained doctors continued to believe in supernatural explanations and cures, or in the influence of the planets.

People continued to rely on **informal healers**, especially housewife-physicians, 'wise women', witches, wizards.

The belief that the **'King's Touch'** cured people of scrofula persisted.

'Cures' based on **bleeding and purging** were common.

PRACTICE

1 Whose book, published in 1628, showed that Galen had been wrong about the heart and the circulation of the blood?

2 What important invention by A. van Leeuwenhoek in 1693 later helped further progress in medical knowledge?

MEDICINE THROUGH TIME

The Industrial Revolution (1)

THE BARE BONES

➤ At the start of the Industrial Revolution, in about 1750, there was little change in medicine.

➤ In fact, the early consequences of the Industrial Revolution were worse – public health problems grew in the new industrial towns.

➤ But later, new technology and chemicals paved the way for important new discoveries.

A The state of medicine by 1750

KEY FACT

1 The seventeenth-century Scientific Revolution had, by the early eighteenth century, led to increased respect for physicians and doctors.

Remember
Increasing professionalism in medicine led to the exclusion of women, even from their traditional role as midwives.

• It had also led to **improved training and standards.** In particular, **surgeons gained equal status with physicians.** As a result, organisations to represent surgeons were set up in Britain and Europe.

• In Britain, in 1745, the Company of Surgeons was set up. **In 1800, this became the Royal College of Surgeons of London.** This led to **improved standards for surgical training.**

• **Several hospitals were established** for the care of the sick: Guy's in 1721, and the Middlesex Hospital in 1745.

KEY FACT

2 Despite the more scientific approach and the search for new knowledge, many old ideas continued during the first half of the eighteenth century.

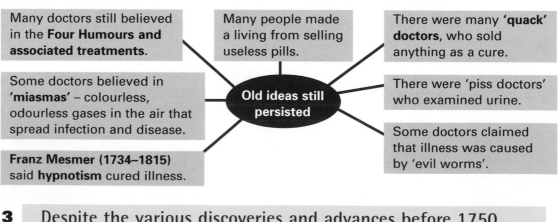

Many doctors still believed in the **Four Humours and associated treatments**.

Some doctors believed in **'miasmas'** – colourless, odourless gases in the air that spread infection and disease.

Franz Mesmer (1734–1815) said **hypnotism** cured illness.

Many people made a living from selling useless pills.

Old ideas still persisted

There were many **'quack' doctors**, who sold anything as a cure.

There were 'piss doctors' who examined urine.

Some doctors claimed that illness was caused by 'evil worms'.

 **Q** Explain the theory of 'miasmas'.

KEY FACT

3 Despite the various discoveries and advances before 1750, doctors still had little knowledge about the causes of disease.

• Most doctors **did not have any knowledge of chemistry or biochemistry,** and physics was still limited. Although **microscopes** had been invented, they **were not very powerful**.

MEDICINE THROUGH TIME

B   The impact of the Industrial Revolution

KEY FACT

1   <u>From about 1750</u>, Britain underwent several changes that soon led to <u>the emergence of an industrial society</u>. This <u>Industrial Revolution</u> had <u>a mixed effect on medicine</u>. In terms of <u>public health</u> in the rapidly growing factory towns, it was, at first, a negative one.

Remember
This period was known as the 'medical revolution' because progress was much more rapid than in the previous three to four thousand years.

There were **no building standards or regulations** – this led to **'gerry building' of slum housing**.

Governments maintained a **laissez-faire attitude** – that is, they believed that there should be **no central government intervention**.

The main problems were caused by **sewage being dumped into rivers, overflowing cesspits and human waste being thrown into the streets**.

There were **frequent epidemics of infectious diseases**, such as influenza, smallpox, typhus and typhoid fever.

In large industrial towns, people lived in **overcrowded areas with poor public health**.

Attempts at providing fresh water and removing sewage and rubbish were **local efforts**. These were **haphazard and insufficient to cope** with the scale of the problem.

Another problem was the **smoke from the closely-packed houses and the factories** (many of the latter also discharged **dangerous chemicals** into the environment).

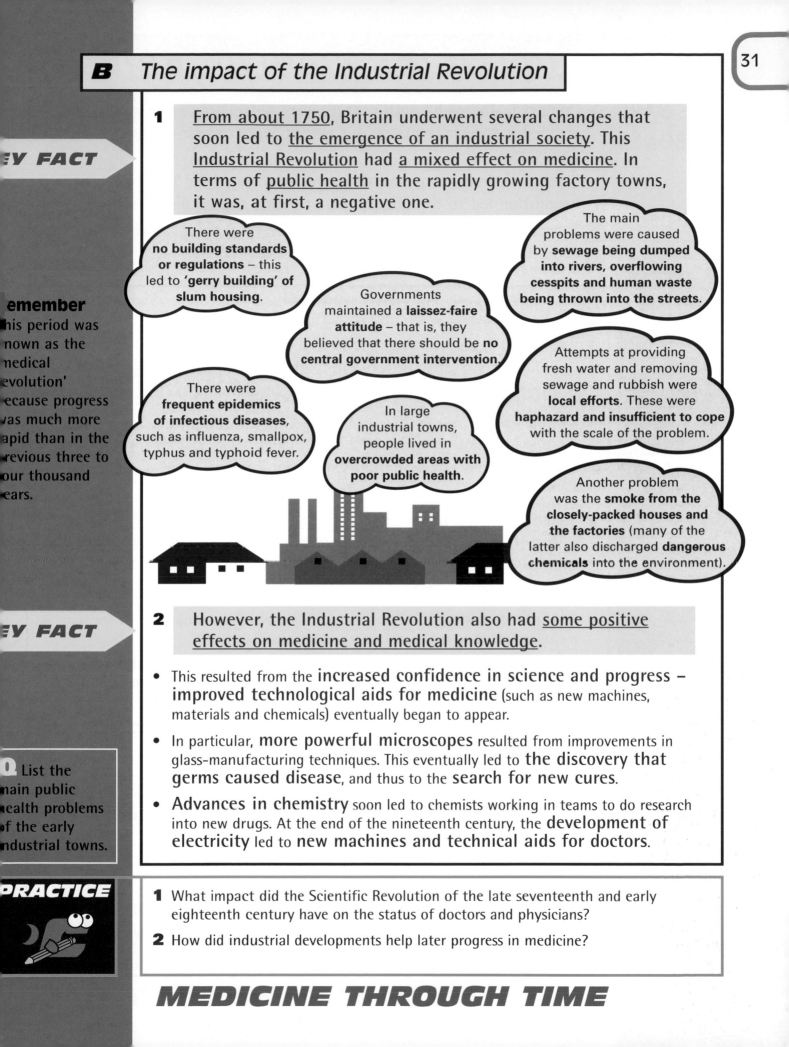

2   However, the Industrial Revolution also had <u>some positive effects on medicine and medical knowledge</u>.

- This resulted from the **increased confidence in science and progress – improved technological aids for medicine** (such as new machines, materials and chemicals) eventually began to appear.

- In particular, **more powerful microscopes** resulted from improvements in glass-manufacturing techniques. This eventually led to **the discovery that germs caused disease**, and thus to the **search for new cures**.

- **Advances in chemistry** soon led to chemists working in teams to do research into new drugs. At the end of the nineteenth century, the **development of electricity** led to **new machines and technical aids for doctors**.

Q List the main public health problems of the early industrial towns.

PRACTICE

1 What impact did the Scientific Revolution of the late seventeenth and early eighteenth century have on the status of doctors and physicians?

2 How did industrial developments help later progress in medicine?

MEDICINE THROUGH TIME

The Industrial Revolution (2)

THE BARE BONES

➤ Doctors in the eighteenth century were better trained in anatomy, chemistry and observation. This helped Jenner make an important discovery.

➤ Later, new technology and chemicals resulting from the Industrial Revolution led to the discovery that germs caused diseases.

➤ Eventually, scientists and doctors discovered vaccines against certain diseases – first in animals, then in humans.

A The significance of Jenner

KEY FACT

1 Edward Jenner (1749–1823) trained under John Hunter. As a result of his close observations of patients, Jenner discovered the method of vaccination against smallpox in 1796.

Q Why did people oppose Jenner's method of vaccination?

- An early method used to fight smallpox was **inoculation** (used in China and Turkey, and brought to England in **1718** by **Lady Mary Wortley Montagu**).

- After years of observation, **Jenner experimented successfully on a boy** called James Phipps.

KEY FACT

2 Jenner called his method vaccination, and published his results in 1798. However, he met much opposition – he was an unknown country doctor and was unable to explain why his method worked.

Remember
It was 80 years before another vaccine was discovered.

- The **Anti-Vaccine Society** was set up, but many people supported Jenner's methods (including the royal family and Napoleon).

- As a result of this support, he **received money from Parliament** which, in 1840, made vaccination free for all infants. **In 1853, the government made vaccination compulsory** – a very unusual step.

B Germs and anti-toxins

KEY FACT

1 By 1800, most scientists and doctors knew that micro-organisms (microbes) existed, but many believed in the theory of 'spontaneous generation'.

Remember
Many believed these organisms were the result not the cause of disease; others that disease was caused by 'miasmas'.

- In 1849, **Louis Pasteur (1822–1895)**, Professor of Chemistry at Strasbourg, began to work as an industrial chemist. **In 1857, by accident**, he became the first to discover **the link between germs and disease** in plants and animals.

- Many scientists and doctors at first refused to accept his discovery but, **in 1867, Pasteur proved another disease was caused by germs.**

MEDICINE THROUGH TIME

B

2 The next important step was taken by a German doctor, <u>Robert Koch (1843–1910)</u> who, building on Pasteur's work and using newer technology, went on to show how <u>a particular germ caused a particular disease</u>.

- By then, **national rivalry** between French and German scientists existed as a result of the Franco-Prussian War 1870–1871. **Each national team tried to be the first to make the next breakthrough.** Governments were prepared to fund research for **national prestige**.

- In 1875, Koch discovered the anthrax microbe. In 1878, he discovered **how germs made wounds go septic in humans**.

- He discovered germs causing TB (1882) and cholera (1883). He did this using a microscope with **a newer and more powerful lens, solid cultures** (better than the liquid ones used by Pasteur), **new chemical dyes and photography**.

- Many other germs were discovered in the 1880s and early 1890s by other scientists.

3 However, despite these discoveries, there was <u>still no cure for those already infected with a disease</u>.

Pasteur and his team discovered a vaccine for chicken cholera using a mild dose of the disease (the principle of **attenuation**). Pasteur went on to find **a vaccine against anthrax in animals**.

One of his teams led by **Dr Emile Roux demonstrated this successfully in public in 1881**. The electric telegraph meant the rest of the world (including Koch) heard of it that same day.

In **1882**, Pasteur set up a team to find a **cure for rabies in animals** using Roux's ideas. **By chance, he was forced to test it on a human in 1885** when a child was bitten by a rabid dog. A series of injections prevented the boy getting the disease. Such breakthroughs gave scientists the **confidence to move on to find vaccines for human diseases**.

The **first cure of an ill human** by the use of an anti-toxin was in **1891 (a child with diphtheria)**. Soon, other anti-toxins were developed.

The **important breakthrough** was made by **Emil von Behring**, one of Koch's assistants. He took a discovery made by Roux (that germs caused diseases by producing **toxins** [poisons] in the blood stream), and found that some animals produced an **anti-toxin to fight the poison**. Behring experimented by **extracting the anti-toxins** and injecting them into humans. These destroyed the poisons caused by the germs.

Q What helped Koch make his discovery that particular germs caused particular diseases?

PRACTICE

1 What was unusual about the British government's reaction in 1853 to Jenner's discovery of vaccination?

2 How did the Franco-Prussian War, 1870–1871, act as a factor stimulating new discoveries concerning germs and diseases?

MEDICINE THROUGH TIME

The drugs revolution (1)

➤ By 1900, the germs that caused the most common diseases had been discovered.

➤ This led to various vaccines against those diseases, and to governments introducing preventative public health measures.

➤ But cures for those already ill were still needed. Progress in this came in the first half of the twentieth century.

A Ehrlich and 'magic bullets'

KEY FACT

1 In 1884, Ilya Metchnikoff had identified antibodies as a natural defence mechanism of the body; and people knew that antibodies attacked specific germs.

- The next important breakthrough was made by **Paul Ehrlich (1854–1915)**. He had worked with Behring as part of Koch's team and became director of his own research team in 1899.

Remember
By about 1890, doctors knew (from the work of Joseph Lister) that a chemical (carbolic acid) could kill germs outside the body, but it was too toxic to be used inside the body.

- Ehrlich called the antibodies produced naturally by the body **'magic bullets'**, as they fought specific germs **without harming the rest of the body**.

- At first, he tried to extract them to cure ill patients, but they did not always work. So he began to look for **synthetic chemical 'magic bullets'** to cure disease.

- As part of Koch's team, he had used **dyes to stain microbes**. After 1899, he tried to see if the dyes would kill the germs. In this, he was **helped by advances in the German chemical industry**, which was producing **synthetic dyes**.

- Although he found dyes that attacked **malaria and sleeping sickness** germs, he **had only limited success at first**.

KEY FACT

2 In 1906, Schaudinn and Hoffman identified the syphilis microbe. In the following year, Ehrlich began to search for a chemical 'magical bullet' to cure this disease.

In 1909, after Ehrlich's team had tested over 600 dyes, **Sahachiro Hata** joined the team. He retested the dyes and found that dye 606 worked – this became known as **Salvarsan 606**.

After testing it on hundreds of animals deliberately infected with syphilis, it was **first tried on a human in 1911**.

However, there was **much opposition to this discovery** – it was difficult and painful to inject and some feared it would encourage promiscuity.

It was **over 20 years before a second 'magic bullet' was discovered** by Domagk in 1932.

Q Why did Ehrlich refer to his drugs as 'magic bullets'?

B Domagk and sulphonamides

1 Gerhard Domagk worked for a large chemical firm in Germany, and had already discovered a cure for sleeping sickness (germanin).

- In 1932, Domagk found that a red dye – **prontosil** – stopped the microbes that caused blood poisoning from multiplying.

- In 1935, Domagk's daughter had blood poisoning. There was little hope of her surviving **so Domagk gave her a large dose of prontosil.**

- **She recovered**, although one **side-effect** was that her skin went bright red.

2 French scientists then identified the active ingredient of prontosil as a sulphonamide, a chemical derived from coal tar.

- This led to a **range of new drugs based on sulphonamides**, including **M&B 693** which acted against **pneumonia**, as well as drugs for **tonsillitis, puerperal fever and scarlet fever**.

- M&B 693 was tested on a man with pneumonia by the British firm May and Baker in 1938. This trial was successful, and the man recovered from his illness.

- These drugs did not turn the patients red, but some had more **serious side-effects** such as damage to the kidneys and the liver.

- These sulphonamides were also **ineffective against the stronger microbes**.

What were ne two main roblems with ulphonamide- ased drugs?

Study Source A below and then answer the question which follows.

Source A An extract about part of the research into the effectiveness of dye 606.

> EHRLICH looked at the records and said, 'No, surely not! It was all minutely tested by Dr R. and he found nothing. More than a year ago we laid aside 606 as worthless. You are sure that you are not mistaken, Dr Hata?'
>
> Hata pointed to the records of the experiments, and said, 'I found that, Herr Direktor'.
>
> 'Then it must be repeated, dear Hata,' said Ehrlich.
>
> The treatment with 606 had amazingly successful results, but Ehrlich demanded that it should be repeated over and over again with hundreds of experimentally infected animals. At length, Ehrlich convinced himself of the outstanding curative power of 606.

Try to give a BALANCED answer – consider the arguments for AND against it being a turning point.

To what extent was Ehrlich's discovery of Salvarsan 606 a turning point in the history of medicine?

MEDICINE THROUGH TIME

The drugs revolution (2)

THE BARE BONES

➤ The problems associated with chemical 'magic bullets' were eventually overcome by the discovery of antibiotics.

➤ The first antibiotic was penicillin, discovered by chance by Alexander Fleming in 1928.

➤ Problems of mass production were not overcome until the Second World War. However, antibiotics have still not eradicated all infectious diseases.

A The work of Fleming

KEY FACT

1 <u>Alexander Fleming</u> was the first to discover a drug – <u>penicillin</u> – derived from a living organism which could kill bacteria, or at least prevent them from growing.

• During the First World War, while working in a military hospital, Fleming had become **interested in how to deal with wounds that became infected**. He noted that the **antiseptics used were not very effective**.

• **In 1922**, Fleming discovered that **lysozyme** (found in tears) killed some germs, but not those causing disease and infection.

KEY FACT

2 In 1928, Fleming began work on <u>staphylococci</u> (germs that make wounds septic). One day, <u>by chance</u>, he noticed that mould was growing on some Petri dishes.

• More importantly, he noticed that **no germs were growing near the mould**. He grew more of it, and **found it killed many deadly germs**.

• A colleague identified the mould as belonging to the **penicillium family**. But, although he **tried to purify** the 'mould juice', the **necessary chemical skills were unavailable**.

KEY FACT

3 After Fleming had tested the mould on animals, and showed it did no harm, <u>he tried it on a colleague's eye infection</u>. Again, it worked, and <u>did no harm to body tissues</u>. This was a big improvement on chemical 'magic bullets'.

Remember
No one was prepared to give Fleming the specialist help or money necessary to try to turn the 'mould juice' into a pure drug.

• **In 1929 and 1931**, he wrote up his research and called the 'mould juice' **penicillin**. Although it seemed much better than the sulphonamide drugs, as it worked on almost all the serious microbes and yet caused no damage to the body, **Fleming did not persist in trying to make pure penicillin**.

• Instead he returned to his more routine work. **Work by others** would be necessary to develop plentiful supplies of this first antibiotic drug using **mass industrial production techniques**.

MEDICINE THROUGH TIME

B After Fleming

Y FACT

1 The next important step in the development of penicillin was taken by <u>Howard Florey and Ernst Chain</u>.

- **Florey** was an Australian doctor and **Chain** was a Jewish scientist who had fled Nazi persecution.
- **In 1938, they decided to study germ-killing substances**. Chain came across Fleming's article on penicillin, and tried to produce pure penicillin.
- A small amount was produced by using **freeze-drying techniques**. The penicillin was tested successfully on mice before being used on humans.

Y FACT

2 <u>Penicillin was successfully tested on a human for the first time in 1940</u>. At first, the patient improved but, when the supplies were used up, he died.

emember
Fleming, Florey and Chain were awarded the Nobel Prize in 1945.

Florey and Chain **did not have the resources to manufacture the drug in large quantities**. When war broke out in 1939, Florey pointed out to the British government how the drug could cure infections in deep wounds.

But the government, and the British chemical industry, were **too involved in making explosives** to provide the resources and facilities needed.

Florey then approached **US chemical firms**. At first, he was unsuccessful, but **after Pearl Harbor in 1941, he was given financial help**.

After the war, **even better methods of mass production** led to reduced costs. Soon, penicillin was used to treat a whole range of diseases.

Mass production of penicillin began in Britain in 1943. By 1944, there was enough penicillin to treat all wounded Allied forces in Europe.

Y FACT

3 However, although penicillin (and other antibiotics) were very successful in fighting many killer infectious diseases, <u>not all were conquered fully</u>.

The overuse of antibiotics **has resulted in** some bacteria being immune – **the so-called** 'super bugs'.

The failures of antibiotics

Many diseases **in developed countries** are not infectious, **such as heart disease and cancer**.

TB has not been wiped out, and is making a come-back **in both the developing and the developed worlds**.

Q Which factors finally allowed the mass production of penicillin?

PRACTICE

1 How did Alexander Fleming first discover penicillin?

2 How important was war as a factor in the development of penicillin?

MEDICINE THROUGH TIME

Medicine now

➤ Since 1900, there have been rapid changes in many areas of medicine. However, several problems have emerged.

➤ The role played by governments in health issues has greatly expanded – most obviously with the establishment of the NHS.

➤ Concerns over cost, and new health problems, have led to a revival of interest in alternative medicine.

A Improvements and problems

KEY FACT

Q What problems have arisen to do with the use of antibiotics such as penicillin?

KEY FACT

Remember
New health problems associated with modern lifestyles (obesity, smoking, poor diet, lack of exercise, cancer clusters close to factories and waste tips, pollution and allergies, and an ageing population) are causing concern.

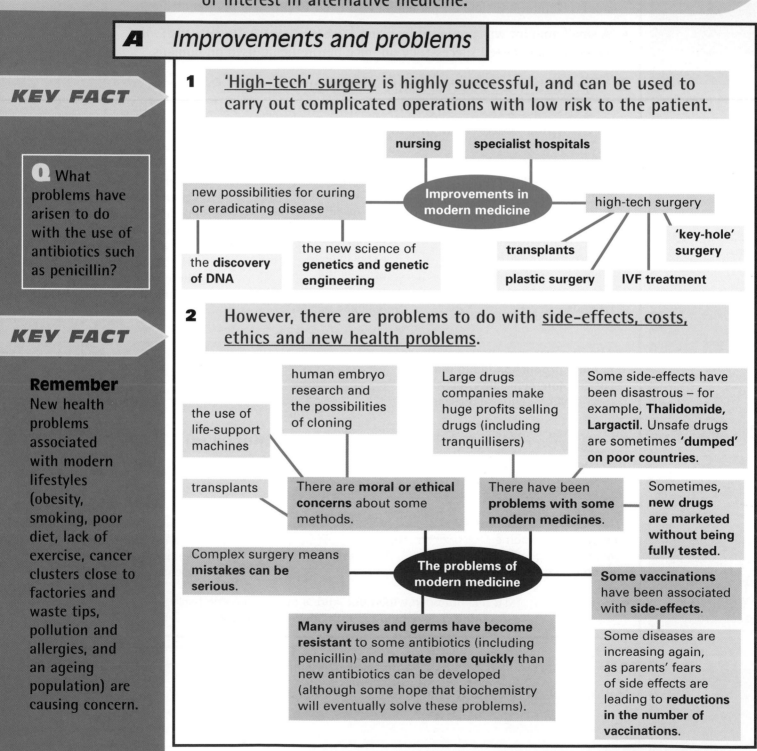

1 'High-tech' surgery is highly successful, and can be used to carry out complicated operations with low risk to the patient.

nursing

specialist hospitals

new possibilities for curing or eradicating disease

Improvements in modern medicine

high-tech surgery

the **discovery of DNA**

the new science of **genetics and genetic engineering**

transplants

'key-hole' surgery

plastic surgery

IVF treatment

2 However, there are problems to do with side-effects, costs, ethics and new health problems.

human embryo research and the possibilities of cloning

the use of life-support machines

Large drugs companies make huge profits selling drugs (including tranquillisers)

Some side-effects have been disastrous – for example, **Thalidomide, Largactil.** Unsafe drugs are sometimes **'dumped' on poor countries**.

transplants

There are **moral or ethical concerns** about some methods.

There have been **problems with some modern medicines**.

Sometimes, **new drugs are marketed without being fully tested**.

Complex surgery means **mistakes can be serious**.

The problems of modern medicine

Some vaccinations have been associated with **side-effects**.

Many viruses and germs have become resistant to some antibiotics (including penicillin) and **mutate more quickly** than new antibiotics can be developed (although some hope that biochemistry will eventually solve these problems).

Some diseases are increasing again, as parents' fears of side effects are leading to **reductions in the number of vaccinations**.

B Changing attitudes and alternative medicine

1 Since 1900, <u>attitudes about the role of government in health care have changed</u>.

- Twentieth-century governments have **intervened increasingly** in areas such as housing and waste disposal.
- **In 1948, the National Health Service** was set up by the Labour government. But **demand was far greater than expected**.
- This caused the NHS serious problems. Soon treatment was **no longer free**, as charges were imposed for eye tests, dental care and prescriptions.
- The **rationing of resources** due to 'high-tech' machines, more expensive drugs and longer life expectancy has led to **longer waiting lists**. Some wealthier people have avoided these problems by taking out **private medical insurance** to get **quicker treatment**.

2 However, 'high-tech' medicine has <u>not led to the disappearance of traditional medicine</u>.

- Interest in **traditional and alternative methods** has increased in Europe, partly as a result of the growing problems of modern medicine.
- Such methods include **herbal medicine** (often using herbalist recipes from the Middle Ages), **'natural cures'** (based on diet and exercise, similar to the Ancient Greeks' idea of 'regimen'), **acupuncture** (using a theory of physiology used by the Chinese for centuries) and even visits to 'faith' or spiritual **healers** of various kinds (similar to the supernatural beliefs of people in the past).
- The number of people turning to such approaches has **increased rapidly** since the 1980s.

emember
everal thousand
aditionally
ualified doctors
ccasionally use
uch alternative
ethods along
ith modern
ethods.

PRACTICE

Study Sources A and B, and then answer the question which follows.

Source A An extract from a school textbook on medicine, published in 1996.

Since the 1940s a number of unknown lethal diseases have developed. AIDS is the best known of these. Others include Lassa fever, Ebola virus, Dengue, Kuru, Machupo and Creutzfeld-Jacob disease.

One reason these diseases can spread rapidly is the ease of travel and communication today. Another reason is that viruses and germs have become resistant to some antibiotics and sometimes mutate more quickly than new antibiotics can be found to combat them.

Source B President Kennedy's request for laws to control the sale of medical drugs, in his message to the US Congress in 1962.

More than 9000 new drugs (have been developed) in the last 25 years. These drugs present new hazards as well as greater benefits than ever before for they are widely used, they are often very potent and they are presented by aggressive sales campaigns that may tend to overstate their merits and fail to indicate the risks involved in their use.

To what extent do Sources A and B agree that modern medical drugs are the major cause of new health problems?

MEDICINE THROUGH TIME

Women and medicine (1)

THE BARE BONES
- ➤ Women were allowed to practise as doctors in the ancient world.
- ➤ Their involvement in medieval European medicine became increasingly restricted.
- ➤ By 1750, the growing insistence on formal education and training meant women only practised informal medicine.

A The situation before 1500

KEY FACT

1 In the civilisations of the ancient world, there were few trained doctors. <u>Most people had to rely on informal (untrained) family or local healers – many of these were women</u>.

Remember
Some midwives were more formally trained as apprentices and became members of a guild.

The role of women in medicine, pre-1500

Women worked in all areas of medicine – as physicians, surgeons and midwives.

In both Ancient Greece and Rome, **midwives were taught by doctors**. Doctors were only called to assist if there was a problem – for example, to perform 'Caesarean section' operations, following a law (Lex Caesarea) passed in the ninth century BC.

In **Ancient Egypt**, some wall paintings show only women **assisting at births**. Others show both men and women.

With the **collapse of Rome**, there was a return to a more primitive approach and a **greater reliance on the informal medicine** practised by family and local healers.

Ancient Egyptian doctors were allowed to **train their daughters in medicine** if they had no sons.

In **Ancient Greece, women were allowed to practise as doctors**. This was linked to the belief that Asclepios, the god of healing, had two daughters – **Hygeia and Panacea** – who helped him 'cure' the sick.

Women doctors were allowed to practise in the Islamic world, particularly as specialist childbirth doctors.

KEY FACT

2 In <u>medieval Europe</u> (as in the Islamic world), it was at first thought improper for male physicians to treat females, so <u>female patients relied on other women</u>.

Q How did women come to be excluded from most areas of medicine during the Middle Ages?

- However, in Europe during the Middle Ages, **the Church** (which controlled education and the universities) **began to make medical training more formal** – for example, medical schools were set up from the late eleventh century.

- There is some evidence to suggest that the **first medical school** in Salerno **trained women doctors**. However, these **doctors probably only treated other women** (especially during childbirth).

- Soon, even the training of apothecaries and barber-surgeons became more specialised. As **women were excluded from most types of formal education**, only men were allowed to train as doctors.

MEDICINE THROUGH TIME

A

- This growing **insistence on formal medical training** led to **women being excluded from all areas of medicine**, apart from patient care. Women who continued to practise medicine could be tried – for example, Jacoba de Felice in 1322.

- However, as most people could not afford a professional doctor, **women continued to play an important informal role** for the majority of people who became ill.

B Developments 1500–1750

1 The greater knowledge of anatomy as a result of the Renaissance after 1500, and the insistence on formal medical training, led to an <u>even greater exclusion of women from universities, and so from medicine.</u>

- Despite this, there **were still a few women surgeons and doctors** during the Renaissance and even into the seventeenth century, but they were becoming **fewer than in the Middle Ages**.

- Women continued to be **pushed out of most areas of formal medicine** during the sixteenth and seventeenth centuries.

- In about **1620, the obstetric (delivery) forceps** were invented. These required good anatomical knowledge to be used safely, so women were gradually excluded even from midwifery.

2 However, as university-trained doctors were relatively scarce and expensive, <u>women continued to play a significant role in medicine for most ordinary people</u> (especially in the countryside, where the majority lived).

- Women still played an **important informal role** during illness as **housewife-physicians and local 'wise women'**, who acted as herbalists, healers, nurses and witches.

- Often, the **lady of the manor** acted as the housewife-physician for people in the village – for example, Lady Margaret Hoby (1571–1633).

- Other **women continued to take an interest in medicine** – for example, **Lady Mary Wortley Montagu brought knowledge of inoculation to Britain** in 1718. However, such individuals were increasingly rare.

KEY FACT

Remember
Women herbalists often gained a knowledge of plants and herbs from cooking and gardening.

KEY FACT

Q What impact did the obstetric forceps have on women's role in medicine?

PRACTICE

1 Why were fewer and fewer women able to practise as doctors during the Middle Ages?

2 Why did the roles of housewife-physician and 'wise woman' not decline during the period 1500–1750?

MEDICINE THROUGH TIME

Women and medicine (2)

➤ After 1750, the number of female midwives and herbalists continued to decline (they were gradually replaced by male apothecaries and pharmacologists).

➤ However, doctors were still scarce and expensive, so women continued to play an important informal role.

➤ Gradually, women began to make a return to formal medicine – first in nursing and then, from the late nineteenth century, as doctors.

A   Developments 1750–1900

KEY FACT

1 **During the Industrial Revolution**, the poorer classes often relied on informal midwives and 'wise-women'.

The **first signs of change came in nursing**, following the work of **Florence Nightingale** during the Crimean War.

Mary Jane ('Mother') Seacole also played an important part in improving nursing care during the war. However, probably because she was a black woman from Jamaica, she was not given much credit, and was **not allowed to work as a nurse in England** after her return.

Other training schools followed. By 1900, there were 64 000 trained nurses.

In **1859**, Florence Nightingale's book, **Notes on Nursing**, was published, and a public fund was launched to raise money for a proper nursing school. The **Nightingale School of Nursing** was based at St. Thomas' Hospital in London.

As a result of these developments, **nursing started to become a respectable medical profession**.

KEY FACT

2 However, there were **still no women doctors** – universities and medical colleges refused to accept women as students.

- **Social attitudes** concerning women's rights to education and employment **began to change** from about 1850.

- Inspired by Elizabeth Blackwell, **Elizabeth Garrett** tried to qualify as a doctor in Britain. Although she was allowed to enrol in the Society of Apothecaries, **no British university would allow her to qualify as a Doctor of Medicine**.

- **Sophia Jex-Blake** (and five other women) **completed a medical course at Edinburgh University in 1874**, but the university said it could only award medical degrees to men. **In 1876**, partly as a result of increasing protests about such inequalities, **all medical qualifications were opened to women**.

Q List the factors that led to women being allowed to train and practise as doctors after 1850.

MEDICINE THROUGH TIME

B Changes since 1900

Y FACT

1 Before 1900, the medical profession was still overwhelmingly dominated by men.

- The one exception to this was nursing. In 1919, the Registration of Nurses Act set out the qualifications needed to enter nursing.
- Nursing became a highly respected profession – many men now choose it as a career.

Y FACT

2 One of the biggest factors leading to greater equality for women in medicine was the impact of two world wars.

- The **First World War** resulted in a greater need for nurses and doctors. This gave **more opportunities for women**.
- As well as large numbers of women working as **nurses, more women acted as doctors and surgeons**.
- The work of **Elsie Inglis, Flora Murray and Louisa Garrett Anderson**, was important in setting a pattern for this.
- Even greater opportunities came with the **Second World War** and the **establishment of the NHS**.

Q What was the impact of war and the NHS on women's involvement in medicine after 1900?

Y FACT

3 Moves to greater equality for women in medicine have also been helped by a series of new laws.

- The **Sex Discrimination Act, 1975**, meant (in theory) that all jobs were to be open to women, including those in medicine.
- However, despite these gains, **women are still under-represented** in the medical profession, especially in the top jobs, such as hospital consultants.

PRACTICE

Study Source A, which is about the position of women in medicine in the period 1750–1900. Then answer the question which follows.

Source A A cartoon of 1796 showing a male midwife.

Make sure that you mention words like 'useful' and 'uses' in your answer.

How useful is Source A in showing the position of women in medicine during the period 1750–1900? Use the source, and your own knowledge, to explain your answer.

MEDICINE THROUGH TIME

THE BARE BONES

➤ In the civilisations of the ancient world, cleanliness had often been seen as important.

➤ The Romans, in particular, achieved important advances in public health.

➤ After the fall of Rome, there was a prolonged regression in this aspect of medicine in Europe for over 1000 years.

A   The ancient civilisations and the Middle Ages

1   In <u>Ancient Egypt</u>, priests washed regularly, changed their clothes frequently and shaved their heads. However, they had no drainage system for toilets, and only the well-off had bathrooms.

- Ancient Egyptian **toilets** were stone seats placed over large jars, which were emptied by slaves. Often, the contents were spread on fields as manure.

- Although there was little change in Ancient Greece, **the Romans did take several important practical measures to ensure better public health** (clean drinking water, public baths and toilets, sewers, drainage of swamps).

2   <u>When the Roman Empire collapsed</u>, such <u>practical, organised measures disappeared rapidly</u> during the 'Dark Ages'.

Even **in the Middle Ages, governments were unwilling to provide public health facilities**. They also often lacked the power, money or authority to enforce such measures.

Instead, **each medieval town was left to itself**, with decisions taken by its **corporation** (made up of rich men). Usually, such corporations were reluctant to spend money, and felt that public health **was not their responsibility**.

While towns were small, there were no major public health problems. But **as trade and towns grew, the risks increased**. Often, rubbish and sewage **piled up in the streets, or was dumped in nearby rivers**.

Although **some towns passed by-laws** – for example, about the regular emptying of cesspits – these were **difficult to enforce**. Usually, **action only followed after a serious outbreak of disease**.

There was **no real understanding of the causes of such epidemics**, or how to prevent them. The worst example was the Black Death (bubonic plague) which first hit Britain in 1348.

KEY FACT

Q. How did public health in Europe regress after the fall of Rome?

KEY FACT

Remember Exceptions to the virtual absence of public health measures in the Middle Ages were the monasteries and church hospitals, which kept alive aspects of Roman methods and inventions (such as water supplies, cleanliness). But this benefited only a few.

B Continuing problems, 1500–1750

EY FACT

Q How did wars in this period contribute to public health problems?

1 There was <u>not much improvement in public health after the Renaissance</u>. <u>Frequent wars</u> and the <u>rising populations of towns and cities</u> placed even <u>greater strains on clean water supplies and sewage disposal systems</u>.

People often tried to build new houses within a town's walls as protection from invaders. This led to **overcrowding, especially in the poorer areas**.

The impact of frequent war

Sieges led to starvation and associated illnesses.

Wars were **very expensive** so there was **no spare money** for public health measures and **governments took little action**.

Armies brought diseases.

EY FACT

Remember
Some steps to deal with the plague showed that people realised that it was contagious, but they did not know how it was spread.

2 As a result of all these problems, outbreaks of <u>plague continued to occur frequently all over Europe</u>.

- In Britain, the worst reappearance was the **Great Plague of London, 1665–1666**, in which over 100 000 people died.

- **Some steps were taken to try to control its spread** – for example, locking those with the disease into their houses.

- The authorities also **paid for bodies to be collected and for mass burials in plague pits**.

- The Great Plague did not really end until the **Great Fire of London in 1666**, which **sterilised large areas of the city**.

PRACTICE

Study Sources A and B below, which refer to the Black Death of 1348–1349, and then answer the question which follows.

Source A An order sent by Edward III to the Lord Mayor of London in 1349, the year after the Black Death arrived in Britain.

To the Lord Mayor of London
An order to cause the human excreta and other filth lying in the streets and lanes in the city and its suburbs to be removed with all speed. Also to cause the city and suburbs to be kept clean … This is so that no greater cause of death may arise from such smells. The king has learnt that the city and suburbs are so full with filth from out of the houses by day and night that the air is infected and the city poisoned.
　　　This is a danger to men, especially by the contagious sickness which increases daily.

Source B People whipping themselves (flagellants) – they believed that God had sent the Black Death because people were sinful and that by punishing themselves, they would persuade God to be merciful.

Make sure you comment on the information provided by BOTH of the sources.

Using the two sources, and your own knowledge, explain what the main problems were concerning public health during the Middle Ages.

MEDICINE THROUGH TIME

THE BARE BONES

➤ The rapid growth of population and towns during the Industrial Revolution led to worsened public health.

➤ This came to a head in the 1840s as a result of cholera epidemics.

➤ Gradually, as a result of improved knowledge and the impact of war, governments took steps to improve public health measures.

A The public health crisis, 1750–1850

KEY FACT

1 Most people believed that governments should follow a laissez-faire policy in most aspects of life.

- As a result, there were **no planning or building regulations**. The result was **overcrowded and bad housing, poor water supplies, and inadequate drainage and sewage disposal.**

- There was also still **no proper scientific/medical understanding of the causes of disease.** Most people believed in 'miasmas' or 'bad air'.

- Consequently, many problems arose from a wide range of **infectious diseases**.

KEY FACT

2 By 1800, some diseases (especially TB, typhus and typhoid) were causing real problems in industrial towns. Then, in 1831, a new disease hit Britain – cholera.

- Some **boards of health** were set up, but were **abolished in 1832**, when it seemed that the epidemic had died out.

- However, the government had been worried by the cholera epidemic, and asked **Edwin Chadwick** to undertake an investigation into the **links between poverty and ill health.**

- Chadwick's **Report**, published in **1842**, recommended **sanitary reform** but led to divided opinions.

KEY FACT

3 Chadwick's findings about the links between poverty, squalor and death rates were later supported by the work of William Farr and Dr Southwood-Smith.

- However, **a Public Health Bill was defeated in 1847** as many MPs opposed the cost and believed that the poor should 'help themselves'. They pointed out that no one actually knew what caused these diseases.

- But then cholera struck again in **1848** – this time, Parliament passed the **Public Health Act**.

- This allowed councils to set up a **General Board of Health** and local Boards of Health, which had the power to improve water supplies and sewage disposal.

Q What were the weaknesses of the 1848 Public Health Act?

B Developments since 1850

KEY FACT

1 Despite the Public Health Act, <u>little changed in most towns</u>.

Remember
Victorian improvements in engineering helped to deal with public health problems – for example, brick-lined sewers and the invention of the flush toilet.

In 1854, **John Snow** discovered the connection between **contaminated water and cholera** by plotting the course of a cholera outbreak in the Broad Street area of London. He noticed that **all the victims used the same water pump**. When he removed the handle from the pump, the epidemic ended.

In the 1860s and 1870s, **the discoveries of Pasteur and Koch about germs** proved that Chadwick and Snow were right.

In 1869, a **Royal Sanitary Commission** investigated the problems associated with water supplies. In response to proposals from **Sir John Simon**, the Medical Officer of Health, the government formed a **Local Government Board (1871)** and divided the country into **'sanitary areas'** administered by **medical officers of health (1872)**.

Another cholera epidemic in 1865–1866 frightened the authorities into taking further steps.

KEY FACT

2 Industrial workers were granted the vote in 1867. This <u>increased the pressure for reform</u>.

- In **1875**, Parliament passed another **Public Health Act** and the **Artisans' Dwellings Act**. However, few slums were knocked down.

- However, this Public Health Act was **more effective**, as it was **now compulsory** for local councils to act on public health matters.

- Further **knowledge about poor living conditions** and their effects was provided by studies carried out by **Charles Booth** in London and by **Seebohm Rowntree** in York.

- This was dramatically underlined by the outbreak of the **Second Boer War in 1899**. Forty per cent of volunteers were rejected as **medically unfit** because of poverty-related illnesses such as rickets and malnutrition.

Q Why was the 1875 Public Health Act more effective than that of 1848?

KEY FACT

3 Greater awareness of public health issues led the <u>Liberal government to begin the creation of the welfare state in 1906</u>.

- The impact of both world wars increased pressure for more reforms. The most important was the introduction of the NHS in 1948 by the new Labour government.

PRACTICE

1 Which disease epidemics in the 1830s and 1840s finally forced British governments to introduce public health reforms connected to water supply and sewage disposal?

2 How did the discoveries of Pasteur and Koch lead to a greater acceptance of the need for public health reform?

MEDICINE THROUGH TIME

Surgery (1)

THE BARE BONES

➤ In the ancient world, some knowledge about the techniques of surgery did exist.

➤ However, there were three major problems associated with surgery – pain, infection and bleeding.

➤ Before 1750, there were no real solutions to these problems. After 1750, some useful progress was made.

A   The main problems of surgery

KEY FACT

1 Despite progress in surgery in the Islamic world (for example, Albucasis), <u>surgery in Europe during the Middle Ages remained limited</u>. Surgeons and barber-surgeons had a low status in the medical profession compared to physicians.

Remember
De Chauliac was helped by improved knowledge of anatomy (for example, Mondino's 'Anatomy' of 1316).

- In fact, **doctors often left surgery to low-paid assistants, and even to untrained barber-surgeons** (local barbers).

- **Some progress** in knowledge was made – **Hugh and Theoderic of Lucca**, for example, discovered the **antiseptic properties of wine** for cleaning wounds in the early thirteenth century, but their ideas did not catch on.

- In **1363**, the French surgeon **Guy de Chauliac** (c.1300–1326), wrote his *Chirurgia Magna*. This became the most important medieval book on surgery.

- In **1376, John of Arderne** used an **early form of anaesthetic** (a mixture of hemlock, opium and henbane), but if the doses were not carefully controlled the patients often died.

KEY FACT

2 <u>Further progress</u> was made in the sixteenth century by the French surgeon, <u>Ambroise Paré (1510–1590)</u>.

- Paré stressed the importance of **first-hand observation** over theory. However, his work had **little impact at the time**.

- In 1534, Paré worked for a public hospital. Then, **in 1537**, he **became an army surgeon** – a position through which he gained much experience.

- But his methods for **cauterising gunshot wounds** (using a cool salve) and **tying off blood vessels** (using double silk threads or ligatures) influenced few doctors – most stuck to traditional methods.

- However, as there were no **antiseptics**, Paré's use of thread **actually increased the chances of wounds going septic** while the **lack of reliable anaesthetics** meant surgery still had to be quick and simple.

- Paré's books (e.g. *Method of Treating Wounds*, 1545, and *Works on Surgery*, 1575) had little influence.

Q Why did some of Paré's discoveries lead to increased death rates?

MEDICINE THROUGH TIME

B Anaesthetics and antiseptics

1 The first of the three major problems of surgery to be solved was that of <u>pain – by the development of anaesthetics</u>.

The discovery of a **reliable anaesthetic** had to wait for the **improvements in the chemical industry resulting from the Industrial Revolution.**

In **1799, Humphrey Davy** (1778–1829) identified **nitrous oxide ('laughing gas')** as a possible solution, but this was **ignored by surgeons at the time.**

In **1847, James Simpson** (1811–1870), Professor of Midwifery at Edinburgh University, discovered the possibilities of **chloroform**, which was easier to administer than ether. However, this **caused liver damage** so surgeons returned to ether after about 1910.

In the USA **in 1842, Crawford Long** discovered the effects of **ether**. Knowledge of this spread to Britain in 1846, and ether was used by **Robert Liston**.

2 However, <u>operations were still carried out in unhygienic conditions</u>.

- **Anaesthetics** allowed longer, more complex operations, **increasing the risks from infection and bleeding. Death rates rose in the 'Black Period' of surgery, 1846–1870.**
- There were no clean, special clothes for surgeons; and no sterilisation of instruments.
- In **1847, Dr Ignaz Semmelweiss**, working in Vienna, ordered doctors to wash their hands (in chloride of lime) before examining patients.
- However, although Semmelweiss' methods led to a dramatic decline in deaths from puerperal fever, **most doctors rejected his idea**.
- In **1861, Pasteur's germ theory was published.** It was read by Joseph Lister, who began to study the infection of wounds in 1865.
- In **1867, Lister used carbolic acid** to disinfect bandages. **In 1871**, he developed a **carbolic spray**.
- This was a **breakthrough** and led to dramatic decreases in deaths from septic wounds. However, **many doctors and nurses disliked the new method.**
- But as a result of **Florence Nightingale's work and better trained nurses**, Lister's idea slowly spread, especially **after 1878**.
- The next important breakthrough came in **1887** in Germany, with the discovery of **asepsis techniques by Professor Neuber and Ernst Bergmann.**
- In **1889** in the USA, **William S. Halsted** developed the idea of rubber gloves, caps, masks and gowns, to protect patients, nurses and doctors.

emember

n important reakthrough in e acceptance f anaesthetics ame when ueen Victoria sed chloroform hile giving rth in 1853.

emember

1878, Koch scovered the acteria causing fection.

Q. How did asteur and och help the evelopment of ntiseptic urgery?

RACTICE

Why were Paré's innovations in surgery not really developed during and after the sixteenth century?

MEDICINE THROUGH TIME

THE BARE BONES

➤ The other major problem of surgery – bleeding – continued unsolved for a long time.

➤ But, in the early twentieth century, with the discovery of blood groups, the problem of bleeding was solved.

➤ Since then, often due to the demands made by modern warfare, surgery has developed rapidly.

A   The impact of war

KEY FACT

1   The idea of <u>blood transfusions</u> was developed in the seventeenth century.

- However, there was a big problem with **clotting**, and patients usually died. Then, in 1901, Karl Landsteiner discovered **blood groups** and the need for compatibility – this led to successful blood transfusions.

- The dreadful injuries of the **First World War** led to the need for more extensive surgery. In 1914, Albert Hustin discovered that **glucose and sodium citrate stopped blood clotting** on contact with air.

- This discovery **allowed blood to be stored more easily. In 1938, the British National Blood Transfusion Service** was set up.

KEY FACT

2   Twentieth-century warfare resulted in a higher proportion of <u>burns injuries</u> than in previous wars. This resulted in the development of a new specialism – <u>plastic surgery</u>.

Remember
Plastic surgery has gone on to become an important specialism in surgery for people suffering from injuries or birth defects.

- **Skin grafting** had been known in Renaissance medicine, but the **problem of infection** meant it was rarely used.

- During the **First World War**, important work was done by **Harold Gillies** to treat burns victims and those suffering from severe facial wounds.

- Gillies set up a special unit to treat such patients, and was the **first plastic surgeon to consider his patients' appearance**.

- Gillies' pioneering work was continued by his assistant **Archibald McIndoe** (from New Zealand) during the Second World War. He used **developments in drugs** (sulphonamides and penicillin) **to prevent infection** when treating airmen disfigured by blazing petrol.

3   During the <u>Second World War</u>, another specialism progressed – <u>heart surgery</u>.

Q Which two surgeons are most associated with the development of plastic surgery?

- Attempts at heart surgery **before the war** were rare.

- US army surgeon **Dwight Harken** cut into beating hearts and used his fingers to remove bullets and shrapnel.

B Modern high-tech surgery

1 A number of important developments have aided modern high-tech surgery, especially the discovery of X-rays by Wilhelm Rontgen in 1895.

More recently, **computerised axial tomography** (CAT) scanners give doctors a 3D image of the whole body.

These are now used in diagnosis, radiotherapy and immunosuppression, the latter being **very important in transplant surgery**.

Progress was made when it was discovered that barium meals allowed X-rays to be taken of the intestines, while **X-ray absorbing dyes** can be injected into the bloodstream.

A breakthrough came **in 1896–1898, when Antoine Henri Becquerel, and Pierre and Marie Curie, discovered the first radioactive isotopes (radium)**.

Developments that aided high-tech surgery

Fibre optics allow doctors to examine the insides of a patient without surgery.

Special microscopes have been developed, along with **very fine sutures and needles**

This has led to **'key-hole' surgery**.

This has allowed the development of **micro-surgery**.

2 Another important specialism is transplant surgery – this has been made possible by a range of discoveries since 1900.

In 1903, **Willem Einthoven** developed the **electro-cardiograph**.

The **first organ transplant was of a kidney in 1951**. This was made possible by the invention **of the first artificial kidney machine** by the Dutch surgeon **Willem Kolff in 1943**.

The **first heart-lung machine was developed in 1953**.

This was achieved by the use of different **immunosuppressants**.

Unfortunately, the patient later died. A temporary halt was called until the **problem of rejection** of the transplanted organ **by the immune system** was solved.

After that, surgeons concentrated on the heart – **Christiaan Barnard** was the first to carry out a heart transplant **in 1967**.

Dr Helen Taussig made important progress in operating on babies with defective hearts (**'blue babies'**).

1 What was the main reason for plastic surgery techniques being developed in the first half of the twentieth century?

2 How did industrial developments help the emergence of high-tech surgery?

MEDICINE THROUGH TIME

THE BARE BONES

➤ In 1783, the USA won its War of Independence against Britain. During the next 50 years, the size of the USA increased greatly as the result of various purchases and deals.

➤ This expansion of the USA led to increasing conflicts with the Native Americans who lived in these new territories.

➤ Several treaties were made – and broken. By 1840, tensions were focused on the Great Plains in the West.

A   The growth of the USA

KEY FACT

1 The first Europeans to settle in the 'New World' were <u>Spanish</u>. Later, came the <u>French, the Dutch and the English</u>.

Remember
The Native Americans were referred to as 'Indians' or 'Red Indians' because Colombus thought he had landed in the Indies in 1492.

- The first European settlements were on the **East Coast**. As the white European populations increased because of immigration, **conflicts developed with the Native Americans** (or Indians) living in the area.

- During the seventeenth and eighteenth centuries, **lands were taken by force** from various Native American nations or tribes. Many were **deliberately infected with European diseases** to which the Indians had no resistance.

- As a result, **many tribes** (such as the Huron, Mohawk, Mohican and Delaware) **were greatly reduced in numbers, or were even wiped out completely**. The Europeans then formed new states in these areas.

KEY FACT

2 <u>In 1775</u>, the 13 East Coast states began a <u>War of Independence</u> against rule by Britain, which had come to control most of North America during the eighteenth century. In 1783, they won their independence.

The **new country of the USA** wanted to expand **westwards**, from the Atlantic in the East to the Pacific in the West.

In **1803**, the USA bought the area known as **Louisiana** from France, for $15 million. It stretched **west from the Mississippi River to the Rocky Mountains**. This area was known as the **Great Plains** and the US government wanted it to be explored. **In 1804, US President Thomas Jefferson** employed **Meriwether Lewis** and **William Clark** to carry out a survey.

In **1819**, the USA also bought **Florida** from Spain. As a result, the USA now owned all the land **east of the Mississippi** as well. But the pressure was now on to move west.

Q What two areas were purchased by the USA in 1803 and 1819 respectively?

THE AMERICAN WEST, 1840-1895

B The Great Plains

1 The <u>Great Plains</u> are in the centre of North America. They were a <u>vast expanse of grasslands</u> with the Low Plains in the East (long prairie grass) and the High Plains in the West (short grass). Those further south were drier and more desert-like.

- The **weather on the Great Plains is often severe**, and still makes farming there in the twenty-first century difficult.

- There are **dry rain shadows** near the Appalachian Mountains in the East and the Rocky Mountains in the West. Many parts of the Great Plains experience **drought in the summer, and heavy snow and extremely low temperatures in the winter**.

2 At first, the early US expeditions west reported that most of the Great Plains was a 'vast inhospitable wilderness' – it was often called the <u>Great American Desert</u>.

- For this reason, US governments were at first prepared to agree to a **Permanent Indian Frontier (PIF)** – that all land west of the Mississippi (which was largely unwanted) could be kept by the Native Americans.

- In **1834**, it was agreed with Native American leaders that all land **west of the 95th meridian** would be **Indian Territory**.

3 However, by the early nineteenth century, many Americans had come to believe there should be one large USA, <u>stretching from the Atlantic in the East to the Pacific in the West</u>.

- Some Americans began to talk of the USA's **Manifest Destiny** to settle west of the Mississippi, and 'civilise' the Native Americans.

- During the 1830s and 1840s, the US government gained other territories – **Texas in 1845, Oregon from Britain in 1846, and California from Mexico in 1848**.

- This meant that the USA now owned **all the land west of the Mississippi**.

- In 1845, the term 'Manifest Destiny' was used to justify what came to be seen as the USA's 'God-given mission' to settle and control all lands in the West, including those promised to the Native Americans.

1 Which US President ordered a surveying expedition of the West in 1804?

2 What new territories did the USA come to control in the late 1840s?

THE AMERICAN WEST, 1840–1895

The Plains Indians (1)

THE BARE BONES

➤ The Great Plains were home to the Plains Indians, who were mostly hunter-gatherers.

➤ There were several different nations of these Native Americans, although they were often organised in a similar way.

➤ One big difference between Plains Indians and white Americans was their system of war.

A Life and organisation

KEY FACT

1 By 1840, the Great Plains was the <u>main area left to Native Americans</u> in North America.

- Those who lived on the Great Plains had heard how the whites had taken lands from the Indians living in the East – many had **accepted refugees**, such as the **Cherokees**, when they were forcibly removed from their lands.

- The stories they heard made many of the Plains Indians **determined to resist** white settlements on their traditional hunting lands.

KEY FACT

2 The Plains Indians belonged to one of several <u>different nations</u>, each of which <u>spoke a different language</u>.

Remember
The Sioux sub-groups were usually referred to by names given to them by Europeans. However, the Sioux called themselves the Lakota, the Nakota and the Dakota (not, respectively, the Teton, Yankton and Santee).

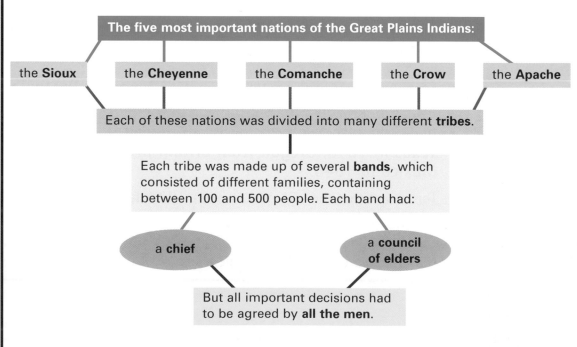

The five most important nations of the Great Plains Indians:

the **Sioux** — the **Cheyenne** — the **Comanche** — the **Crow** — the **Apache**

Each of these nations was divided into many different **tribes**.

Each tribe was made up of several **bands**, which consisted of different families, containing between 100 and 500 people. Each band had:

a **chief**   a **council of elders**

But all important decisions had to be agreed by **all the men**.

Q. Name the five most important nations of the Plains Indians.

- Two other nations were the **Kiowa and** the **Arapaho. Several of the nations were often allies** – for example, the Sioux, Cheyenne and Arapaho, and the Comanche, Kiowa and Apache.

THE AMERICAN WEST, 1840-1895

B Beliefs and warfare

1 Although the different nations of the Plains Indians were often allied, <u>war between them was also common</u>.

- Success in war was of particular importance to each tribe, as well as to individual warriors. In the main, wars consisted of **short, fierce battles** which were fought to **steal horses or captives** (who were kept as family slaves for a time).

- However, because they were nomadic hunters, the aim of war was not to conquer tribes or land – it was for **honour**, which was achieved by proving **courage and bravery**.

- There were strict **codes of honour** in warfare. Especially prized was **counting coup** – this involved running or galloping up to the enemy and touching him with the end of a **coup stick** (about two and a half to three metres long, and usually decorated with feathers).

- The decision to go to war was a very serious one. The **Cheyenne**, for example, usually made decisions about war in a special **council of war chiefs**.

- Before the coming of the whites and 'total war', warfare on the Great Plains was **low-intensity** and **'sustainable'**, with not much emphasis on killing.

2 Another reason warfare on the Great Plains did not result in heavy casualties amongst the Indian tribes was <u>due to the weapons they used</u>.

- Their main weapons were **tomahawks, war clubs** and, especially important, **lances**. The **bow and arrow** was also used for both warfare and hunting.

- To make these weapons, **good quality wood** was used (mainly yew or ash), with **sharpened flint or bone** used for arrow heads, lance heads, or for cutting edges.

Study Source A, and then answer the question which follows.

Source A An extract from a book about the Cheyenne, published in 1978.

> War has been transformed into a great game in which scoring against the enemy often takes precedence over killing him. The scoring is in the counting of coup – touching or striking an enemy with hand or weapons…
>
> A man's rank as a warrior depends on two factors: his total 'score' in coups, and his ability to lead successful raids in which Cheyenne losses are low. Actual killing and scalping get their credit, too, but they do not rate as highly as the show-off deeds.

What can you learn from this source about the differences between the methods of warfare used by the Plains Indians and by whites?

THE AMERICAN WEST, 1840–1895

The Plains Indians (2)

THE BARE BONES

➤ Each Native American nation and tribe had its own complex culture and social structure.

➤ Hunting, especially the buffalo, was central to their way of life and existence, and they had great respect for the environment.

➤ They also had strong religious beliefs, and religious ceremonies played an important part in everyday life.

A Life and hunting

KEY FACT

1 The Plains Indians believed that the <u>tribal homelands belonged to the people as a whole – and to future generations – not to individuals or families.</u>

Q How did the Indians' attitude to land differ from that of most whites?

• As hunting was vital to the Indians' survival, they saw their **hunting lands as sacred** – no one could buy, sell or fence them off. This attitude was **very different from that held by most whites**.

• Family life was based on the fact that the Plains Indians were **hunters who moved frequently** in search of game. They lived in **tepees (or lodges)**.

KEY FACT

2 Most marriages were <u>monogamous</u>, and were usually <u>arranged by the families</u> concerned.

Remember
Many of the ancestors of the Plains Indians had come from the East, where they had originally been farmers. They had been forced west by the expansion of the whites, and had been forced to become hunters.

Old people
• Old people were **cared for and respected for their wisdom**.
• In return, they made sure they were not a burden on the tribe when they became infirm.

Boys
Boys were trained to hunt and fight.

Girls
Girls were taught how to perform household tasks.

Men
• Some tribes allowed a man to have more than one wife – **usually so that he could marry a widow** so that she and her children were looked after.
• The **clearly defined role for men** was to hunt and fight.

Women
• The **clearly defined role for women** was to take charge of all domestic matters and moving camp.
• Women made most of the **finished goods and owned them** – this gave them some **power**.

KEY FACT

3 The Indians' life revolved around the <u>hunting of buffalo</u>. In the early 1800s, there were about <u>60 million</u> buffalo.

• Although the Plains Indians hunted other creatures, **their life centred on the buffalo** and the horses that they rode during the hunts.

THE AMERICAN WEST, 1840-1895

B Religion and beliefs

EY FACT

Remember

On death, the Plains Indians believed people's spirits went to the Happy Hunting Ground – they did not believe in a separate heaven and hell. They also believed that their ancestors' bodies had become dust on the Plains, thus making their tribal lands sacred.

1 The Plains Indians had a <u>strong sense of community and the environment</u>, based on their belief that humans were one part – but only one part – of all the other elements of the natural world.

- The various nations had **different creation beliefs**. Some believed in one 'Father of Life' or 'The Great Spirit'. The Lakota Sioux, for example, worshipped one 'Great God' known as **'Wakan Tanka'**.

- However, most tribes did not believe there was just one supreme being, **but all believed that each creature had a place in nature**. Therefore it was wrong to kill more than you needed, or to pollute the environment.

- They believed that **all elements of the natural world were connected, and contained spirits**, and did not believe that humans were more important than other creatures.

- Many believed that there were **three parallel worlds** – the earth, the water below, and the sky above.

- They also believed that **nature worked in circles** – the sun, the seasons, and life itself. So **circles became important symbols** –tepees were round, villages were built in circles, and even dances took the form of a circle.

2 Each tribe had people who had <u>special religious powers</u>. These holy men were known as <u>shamans or medicine men</u>.

- Shamans and medicine men played an important part in the lives of the Plains Indians, and they **usually conducted the many important ceremonial and religious dances**, such as those before a hunt.

- These rituals and dances – and worship in general – were intended to **keep the tribe in harmony with the spirits of the natural world** that were important to their life, such as buffaloes, bears and antelopes.

- Some ceremonial dances, such as the **Sun Dance**, were especially important and were intended **to protect the tribe**. Some Oglala Sioux men pierced their bodies as part of such religious ceremonies.

- Shamans also tried to **cure those who fell ill or were injured**, often based on the belief of possession by **'evil spirits'**. 'Cures' were attempted by the use of medicine, chants and dances.

- But they also used **traditional practical cures and remedies**, using herbs, animal fats, bark and mosses as ointments and potions.

EY FACT

Remember

Tribe members often undertook fasting and prayer (and even self-torture) to receive 'visions' from the spirits – these were then interpreted by the shamans.

Q What is a shaman?

PRACTICE

1 Why were buffalo so important to the Plains Indians?

2 What was the purpose of the Sun Dance?

THE AMERICAN WEST, 1840–1895

THE BARE BONES

➤ The first Europeans to explore the West were the 'mountain men' pioneers involved in the fur trade.

➤ By 1840, land shortages and a financial crisis in the East led to many whites wanting to move West.

➤ Many of the 'mountain men' helped 'blaze' trails for these early settlers.

A Early pioneers

KEY FACT

Remember
In the early years, many mountain men, who lived a similar life to the Native Americans, married Indian women.

KEY FACT

1 The first steps in opening up the West to Europeans were taken by <u>those involved in the fur trade</u> as trappers, hunters and traders.

• These fur trappers and traders were often known as **mountain men**. They faced **many hazards – severe weather** and **wild animals**, such as bears and wolves.

• Although there was sometimes conflict with Native Americans, **relations were usually good** in the early years.

• This was because the activities of the mountain men **did not disrupt or threaten the Native Americans' way of life**.

2 These early mountain men sometimes worked on their own, and sometimes with others. The more famous ones included <u>Jim Bridger, Kit Carson and James P. Beckwourth</u> (Beckwourth was the first Black American to become famous in the West).

• But, by the early 1830s, most were working for one of **two large fur companies** – the American Fur Company or the Hudson's Bay Company.

• **By 1840, however, the fur trade was declining**. This was the result of changing fashions and the over-hunting of beavers, which resulted in a sharp drop in numbers.

• Soon, **the number of mountain men** acting as fur trappers and traders **declined rapidly**.

• After the collapse of the fur trade, many mountain men stayed in the West to act as **scouts, guides or miners**. Many of them helped **'blaze' the first trails** (routes) **across the Great Plains** to new areas in the West.

Q Why did the number of mountain men working in the West as fur trappers and traders decline after 1840?

THE AMERICAN WEST, 1840-1895

B Wagons and the West

1 Trailblazers opened up the West to a huge wave of settlers who, after 1840, began to follow them. The most famous early trails were the Santa Fe Trail and the Oregon Trail.

- By 1840, there were many who wanted to move west. **In 1843, the great migration to Oregon began.**

A financial crisis in the East in **1837** had ruined many businesses and hit farming.

The US government **promised land** to settlers as part of the belief in **Manifest Destiny**.

Reasons for moving west

There was a **land shortage in the East,** while land was cheaper and more plentiful in the West.

The US government printed **10 000 copies of the map of the Oregon Trail** (made by Fremont) in **1844** in order to encourage even more settlers to go west.

2 As a result, thousands more crossed the Great Plains in the 1840s to make a new life in Oregon or California. By 1848, nearly 15 000 settlers had gone west.

A Most settlers travelled in covered wagons (pulled by oxen, mules or horses), as part of a **wagon train** led by a **pilot** and his **scout**.

C To avoid winter blizzards, **most journeys began in late April/early May**. Journeys took about **four and a half months**.

E The US government then sent troops to protect the settlers, and **built forts along the trails** on Indian lands.

D At first, **most Plains Indian tribes traded** with the white **migrants** as they were only crossing their lands to get to Oregon or California. **But when the numbers of settlers increased, tensions grew.**

B There were **many hazards** – weather, disease, buffalo stampedes, shortages of food and water.

Study the map, and then answer the question which follows.

How did the opening up of the first trails by the early trailblazers affect the development of the West?

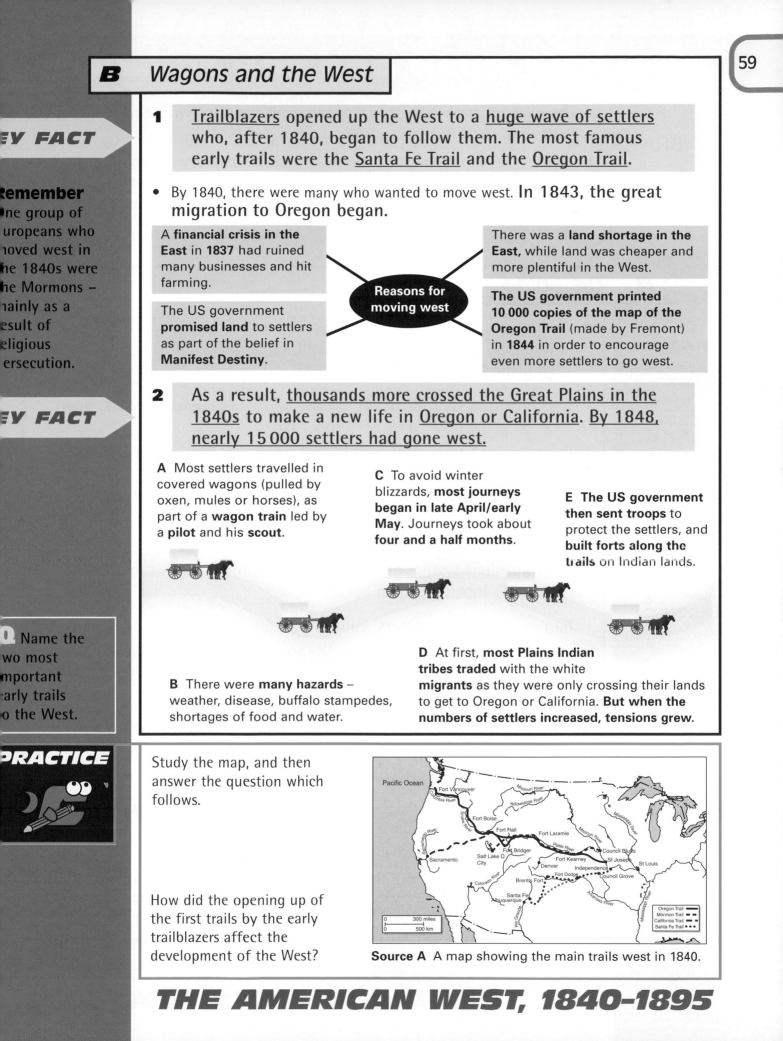

Source A A map showing the main trails west in 1840.

THE AMERICAN WEST, 1840–1895

THE BARE BONES

➤ The next important factor in opening up the West was the 1849 California Gold Rush.

➤ This led to large new settlements, which needed a wide range of services.

➤ The people in these areas also wanted quicker transport. This eventually led to the coming of the railroads.

A The Gold Rush

KEY FACT

Remember
When it became more difficult to extract deposits near the surface, large mining companies and corporations took over.

1 The <u>discovery of gold</u> by Henry Bigler and James Marshall <u>in 1848</u> at Sutter's Mill, <u>California</u>, led to thousands flocking there in 1849.

- This **California Gold Rush** was followed by later discoveries (of gold or silver) elsewhere in the 1850s, 1860s and 1870s.
- The early miners were a **cross-section** of society, and there were also **many from other countries**.
- The early miners used **basic technology** in what was known as **'placer' mining**, using just shovels and pans.

KEY FACT

Remember
Many conflicts were settled democratically, without violence.

2 Because the mining took place in remote places, with <u>no established system of law and order</u>, miners often took matters into their own hands.

- Their set up their own **miners' courts**, often using **brutal** methods.
- Early mining towns were **dirty and disease-ridden**, with plenty of gambling and prostitution. Many soon became **ghost towns** when the gold deposits were exhausted and the miners moved on.

KEY FACT

Q How did the Gold Rushes of the 1840s and 1850s affect relations between whites and the Plains Indians?

3 The great numbers rushing to the gold mining camps in the West <u>needed a wide range of services</u>.

- This demand **stimulated the development of the West**.
- It also encouraged both the US government and businessmen to **expand and improve transport** to the West.
- **Roads** were improved, and **new towns** grew up along the routes.
- But the mining, the influx of travellers and the expansion of transport **increasingly disrupted the way of life of the Plains Indians**. Tension increased when the **US government built forts** to protect the miners.

THE AMERICAN WEST, 1840–1895

B The railways

1 After defeating Mexico and taking California <u>in 1848, nationalism increased in the USA</u>.

- Belief in Manifest Destiny led the US government to **finance mapping and surveying**, and to **subsidise shipping and stage-coach lines**.
- Attempts to **improve communications and transport** between East and West included **steamboats** and **sea travel**, but these were still slow and costly.
- In **1858, the Butterfield Overland Mail** began carrying passengers and post. It cut the journey from East to West to **25 days**.

2 As miners and settlers in the West increased, the US government began to see a <u>transcontinental railroad</u> as a way of <u>uniting the country</u>.

A The US army began surveying possible routes, but from 1861 the Civil War closed off southern routes so a **central** one was chosen.

B Routes through the mountains were difficult so **large numbers of Chinese workers** were brought in (but they suffered bad treatment and prejudice). Once the Civil War ended in 1865, more workers (**often Irish**) came west. Temporary **shanty towns** grew up.

C Two companies were set up – the **Central Pacific Railroad** (starting in California) and the **Union Pacific Railroad** (starting in Omaha). The government helped by giving **generous loans, grants, and land** next to the tracks (often later sold to settlers).

D On 10 May **1869, at the Golden Spike Ceremony**, the two lines met at Promontory Point, Utah. From 1870, other main rail routes were established across the West, such as the **Southern Pacific Railroad** and the **Northern Pacific Railroad**.

3 The construction of the railroads <u>helped the West develop</u> even more extensively.

Thousands of farms were created close to the rail routes. This especially helped **homesteaders on the Great Plains**.

Railroads and the development of the West

Cities connected or close to the railways (such as Los Angeles, Dallas and Denver) grew quickly.

Cattle ranching and the cattle industry benefited and this led to the **growth of cow towns** such as Abilene and Dodge City.

Trade and industry profited as raw materials and finished products for export could now be transported easily.

1 When was gold first discovered in California?

2 What event forced the US government and railroad companies to decide on a central route for the first transcontinental railroad?

THE AMERICAN WEST, 1840–1895

Cattle and cowboys

THE BARE BONES

➤ The early cattle trade began in south Texas. When the railroads came, many in the cattle trade made great fortunes.

➤ Cowboys drove millions of cattle across the Great Plains on what became known as the 'Long Drive'.

➤ Later, cattle ranches were set up, but the cattle boom ended in the late 1880s.

A Early cattle industry

KEY FACT

1 By 1845, when Texas became part of the USA, there were large herds of unclaimed cattle, descended from cattle that had escaped.

Remember
Cattle towns, such as Abilene and Dodge City, grew up quickly.

- These were the **Texas Longhorns** – they were hardier than other breeds, well-suited to being driven long distances over rough country and immune to Texas fever.
- At first, because it was too difficult to transport cattle to the big cities in the East, and the population in the West was so low, there was **little incentive to round these cattle up**.
- Before 1861 and the start of the Civil War though, there were some limited attempts to drive cattle along the **Shawnee Trail to the Mississippi ports**.

KEY FACT

2 By the time the Civil War ended in 1865, there were about five million Texas Longhorns. Most were still unbranded and so could be taken by almost anyone.

- By then, the USA was undergoing an **industrial revolution in the towns of the North–East**. This, plus the growing numbers of soldiers, miners and settlers in the West, led to a **greatly increased demand for meat**.
- More and more railroads were pushing West – this made it much **easier to transport cattle to the East**.
- Cattle that could be bought for about $3 could be sold there for about $30. So the Longhorns were rounded up and driven on the **Long Drive** north to railhead towns.

KEY FACT

3 The most important early cattle trails were the Chisolm, the Sedalia (formerly the Shawnee),and the Goodnight–Loving.

- In 1867, 35 000 cattle were driven north. By 1871, this had risen to **over 600 000 each year**.
- Later, other cattle towns emerged, such as **Dodge City**. Cattle came here via the **Western Trail**, which soon overtook the Chisolm Trail.

Q Name the most important cattle trails.

THE AMERICAN WEST, 1840-1895

B Ranching on the Great Plains

KEY FACT

Remember
Cattle on the Plains increased from 100 000 to four million, 1860–80.

KEY FACT

Remember
Cowboys relaxing after the Long Drive sometimes created disorder and lawlessness, but this has been greatly exaggerated.

KEY FACT

1 During the 1860s and 1870s, many people began to raise cattle on the 'open range' of the Great Plains in order to avoid the Long Drive. Cattle ranching soon spread.

- This was the result of many factors: **railroads extending their networks** west and north; the **development of cold storage and refrigerator cars** on trains; and **new healthier and meatier breeds**.

- **Many huge ranches** soon appeared on the 'open range', and the **massive profits** attracted even more people into cattle ranching.

2 The work on the Long Drive and, later, on the ranches, was done by cowboys.

At first, cowboys came from Texas, but soon they came **from all over the USA**. After the Civil War, they included black Unionist veterans and ex-slaves.

The life of a cowboy

As cattle ranching spread, **some cowboys became more settled**, working on one ranch. However, the work was still hard and low paid – in 1883, **cowboys in Texas went on strike**.

Life and work on the **Long Drive** was hard, with low wages and poor food. The equipment needed (saddles, boots, chaps) was expensive, but had to be provided by the men themselves.

The Long Drive could take up to **four months** from Texas to Abilene. The long hours, dangers and boredom often resulted in quarrels.

There were **many hazards** for a cowboy, including stampedes, river crossings, blizzards, drought and Indian raids. There were also **conflicts with homesteaders, and white rustlers or robbers** (Jayhawks).

3 Although the cattle industry was still booming in the early 1880s, it began to collapse in the late 1880s.

- Many smaller farmers were taken over by **large ranching corporations, led by cattle 'barons'** who formed **powerful associations**.

- Then cattle became more expensive, while beef prices dropped because of **over-production. Overstocking** on the Great Plains led to a reduction in fodder, while **fencing was expensive**.

- There were also **two terrible winters in 1886 and 1887**. Although the cattle industry continued, **the boom was over**.

PRACTICE

Describe the main problems faced by cowboys on the Long Drive.

THE AMERICAN WEST, 1840–1895

Homesteaders

➤ Before the American Civil War, early settlers going west and wishing to farm had headed for Oregon or California.

➤ However, during the 1860s, the US government began to encourage people to settle on the Great Plains.

➤ So larger numbers headed west, but they faced many problems.

A Farming and life

KEY FACT

1 <u>By 1895, there were nearly 450 000 new homesteads (small farms) on the Great Plains. There were many reasons why the numbers of settlers increased greatly during the 1860s.</u>

Q What were the main points of the Homestead Act of 1862?

- **Land** continued to be **scarce and expensive in the East**, while many were seeking a **more prosperous life**, or were trying to **make a new life** after the Civil War.

- The US government also tried to encourage this, by passing the **Homestead Act in 1862**. This led to the biggest growth in farming in US history, with over 65 per cent of farms resulting from the 1862 Act.

> *Homestead Act, 1862*
> *All heads of households, and all males over 21, can have* ***160 acres*** *in the West if they:*
> * *build a* ***house (homestead)*** *on their plot, and*
> * *work on it for* ***five years.***
>
> *They have to pay either:*
> * *a* ***$10 entry fee,*** *or*
> * ***$1.25 per acre.***

KEY FACT

2 <u>However, there were many problems.</u> The price was too high for many ordinary people, and 160 acres was too small.

Remember
Despite the new acts, much of the land was eventually bought up by speculators and the big ranchers.

- As a result, **speculators and railroad companies** bought up most of the best land. **Genuine homesteaders** were left with poor land in remote areas.

- The government eventually tried to improve matters by **passing new acts**, especially **The Timber Culture Act, 1873** and **The Desert Land Act, 1877**.

- The **coming of the railroads** also helped attract homesteaders to the West. Many rail companies sold land granted to them by the government to settlers.

- More importantly, the improved railway network meant **crops could be transported quickly and cheaply** to the big cities in the East or for export.

Timber shortages meant many homesteaders lived in **dugouts or sod houses**.

Difficulties included lack of water, poor soil, insects, and extreme climate variations.

Life for the early homesteaders

Women had many responsibilities. As well as helping with heavier farming work during busy times, they were in charge of the children, the house, clothing, cooking, growing vegetables and tending smaller animals.

Life was very isolated. Doctors were scarce, so childbirth etc., was often faced alone.

Q What were the main problems faced by the early homesteaders?

All tasks were very time-consuming. There was no running water, and women even had to make their own soap. Women also had to collect buffalo chips (dung) for fuel.

THE AMERICAN WEST, 1840–1895

B Later developments

1 The early homesteaders on the Great Plains (known as 'sodbusters') planted wheat and corn. <u>However, their farming methods were more suited to the better climate and fertile soil of the East.</u>

• From 1870, several developments made life easier and farming more **profitable** for thousands of homesteaders.

PROBLEM	**PROBLEM**	**PROBLEM**
The growth of cattle ranching on the 'open range' meant herds often ruined crops. **Wood was too scarce and expensive for fencing**, leading to conflicts between ranchers and homesteaders.	A lack of water	Farming techniques from the East that were not suited to the West.
SOLUTION	**SOLUTION**	**SOLUTION**
In **1874, barbed wire was invented** and was soon mass-produced (but although barbed wire was popular with homesteaders, many ranchers objected).	A constant **drop in the price of wind pumps** which, at first, had been too expensive for most homesteaders, solved this problem. By the 1890s, they had dropped to $25. These pumps meant **deep wells** could be dug, **allowing irrigation which overcame the drying** winds of the Great Plains.	**'Dry farming'** techniques (via deep ploughing) and, by the **early 1880s**, the **use of hardier wheats** (Turkey red – brought by Russian immigrants) made farming easier. Also, **during the 1870s and 1880s, the Industrial Revolution** in the East meant **cheaper and better mass-produced farming equipment**.

2 Identify two developments which, after 1870, made farming on the Great Plains easier for most homesteaders.

PRACTICE

Study Source A, and then answer the questions which follow.

Source A
A woman collecting buffalo dung for fuel.

1 What name was usually given to the buffalo dung used as fuel by the homesteaders?

2 Name two tasks (other than the one shown in the photograph) for which women homesteaders were usually responsible.

THE AMERICAN WEST, 1840–1895

Law and order

THE BARE BONES

➤ In the nineteenth century, the USA had two systems of government. This affected the maintenance of law and order in remote and isolated areas.

➤ The rapid development of the West after 1840 also added to the problems of lawlessness.

➤ However, the problems of outlaws and range wars were eventually solved, bringing an end to the 'Wild West'.

A Early law enforcement

1 Law and order in the USA in the nineteenth century was shared between the <u>federal government</u> in Washington DC, and the various states that made up the USA. Each state had its own governor and government.

- To become a state, a new area was first termed a **US Territory**. It needed at least 60 000 inhabitants before it could become a state. Until then, the governor and top officials were **appointed by the federal government.**

- Territories and states were sub-divided into **counties and towns, each with their own law officers** (sheriffs and town marshals respectively).

2 According to novels and films, the 'Wild West' was full of violence and lawlessness, with <u>gunfights, and stagecoach and bank robberies</u> round every corner.

KEY FACT

Remember
Local law officers also acted as Deputy Federal Marshals.

KEY FACT

Remember
US (Federal) Marshals had authority over all Territories and states, and dealt with train robberies, Indian reservations and army deserters.

Q What was the difference between a US Territory and a state?

The image of the Wild West in novels and films is **an exaggeration.** As the nineteenth century progressed, and settlements grew, the West **began to quieten down.**

There were law and order problems in some areas, **especially in the early mining and cattle towns,** such as Tombstone, Deadwood, Dodge City and Abilene.

Because the Territories were governed from Washington, **decisions were often slow.** The **size** of Territories and states in the West made it hard to establish settled government at first.

The media image of the **Wild West**

The **quick settlement and development of the West** made it difficult to govern at first. Often, such places had no official law officers. When they did, they were sometimes **corrupt or even involved in crime.**

A lack of settled government often led people in such areas to form **miners' 'courts' or vigilance committees,** and to take the law into their own hands. These **vigilantes** carried out punishments which included **lynchings** – sometimes of genuine criminals (and corrupt law officers), but also of innocent people.

THE AMERICAN WEST, 1840-1895

B Outlaws and range wars

1 Although much of the violence of the 'Wild West' was exaggerated, there were some serious problems. Some of the most famous involved <u>gunslingers and outlaw gangs</u>.

- The problems of **distance and travel**, and the **lack of suitable law officers** in the West, made it relatively easy for those wishing to rob or murder.
- Sometimes, wealthy cattlemen hired **gunslingers** in their disputes with homesteaders. However, most gunslingers killed other criminals rather than ordinary citizens.
- There were several **infamous gunslingers and outlaw gangs**, such as Butch Cassidy, the Sundance Kid and the Wild Bunch; Jesse James and the James-Younger Gang; and Billy the Kid.
- There were also several women outlaws – Belle Starr, Etta Place (part of the Wild Bunch), Jennie 'Little Breeches' Metcalf and 'Cattle Annie' McDougal.

2 There were also serious conflicts on the 'open range' between <u>cattlemen and homesteaders</u>. Some developed into full-scale <u>range wars</u>.

- Such violent disputes happened for a **number of reasons** – destruction of crops by cattle, disagreements over water access and water rights, and disputes about land ownership once permanent ranches were being established.
- In **1877–1881**, there was the **Lincoln County War** in Lincoln County, New Mexico. This was between John Chisum (owner of a large ranch) and Lawrence Murphy (a small rancher).
- In **1892**, there was the **Johnson County War**, in Wyoming. By then, the cattle boom was over because of overproduction and the winters of 1886 and 1887.
- But **the cattle barons** blamed the small ranchers and the homesteaders whose barbed-wire fences had ended the open range. The cattle barons in Johnson County formed the **Wyoming Stock Growers' Association** and got a local law passed in 1888 known as the **Maverick Bill**.
- From **1889–1891**, several homesteaders were killed. In **1892**, the cattlemen hired a private army, known as **the Regulators**, but the settlers fought back. Although none of the cattle barons or Regulators were convicted, their power was broken.

KEY FACT

Remember
Even some of the most famous lawmen in the West were a bit dubious, such as Wyatt Earp and his brothers Virgil and Morgan, 'Wild' Bill Hickok and Bat Masterson.

KEY FACT

Remember
There were other bodies involved in maintaining law and order. These included the Texas Rangers, and private detective agencies, such as the famous Pinkerton Detective Agency.

What were the two most important range wars?

PRACTICE

1 Give one reason why law and order was a problem in the West in the early years.

2 What were US Territories?

THE AMERICAN WEST, 1840-1895

> ➤ The conflict between Native Americans and whites, which had grown since US independence in 1783, deepened after 1840.

> ➤ After decades of misunderstanding and white racism, the Plains Indians decided to resist the growing threat to their existence.

A Clash of cultures

1 Native Americans and whites had <u>completely different attitudes towards nature and the land</u>. From the 1850s, the <u>expansion of mining, farming and railroads in the West developed into a war for control of the Great Plains</u>.

KEY FACT

Remember
US governments frequently broke the 1832–1834 agreements with the Indians to give whites access to land west of the PIF.

- When **white Europeans** first settled in the East, they soon **forced out** the Native Americans who had lived there for centuries.

- In **1825**, the US government set aside an area for Native Americans called the **Indian Territory** (in present-day Oklahoma).

- In **1832**, because the US government thought the Great Plains were **useless**, the Native Americans were also 'awarded' these. In **1834**, the border between the USA and the Indian Territory was fixed on the 95th meridian, and was known as the **Permanent Indian Frontier (PIF)**.

2 All land west of this border (mostly the Mississippi River) was to be <u>one huge 'Indian Reservation'</u> where Native Americans could live as they wanted.

KEY FACT

Remember
Over 2000 Cherokees died on their 'Trail of Tears' in 1838–1839.

- In 1830, the **Indian Removal Act** said Indians had to leave all the fertile wooded lands east of the Mississippi.

- The **'Five Cultured Tribes'** (the Cherokee, Creek, Chickasaw, Choctaw and Seminole) were then forced by the US army to move west to a semi-desert region.

KEY FACT

3 During the 1840s, <u>most Indians of the Great Plains did not object</u> to white settlers crossing Indian territory on their way to the new US territories along the Pacific.

Q What were the main points of the 1832 and 1834 agreements made by the US government with Native Americans?

- However, **from the mid-nineteenth century, this began to change**. First, the numbers of miners and settlers crossing their lands increased greatly. Then, the US government began to encourage whites to settle on the Great Plains.

- As attacks by Native Americans on wagon trains and miners' camps increased, **the US government dropped the policy of 'one big reservation'**.

- Instead it decided that the Great Plains Indians **should not stand in the way of Manifest Destiny and the development of the West**.

B Growing conflict

1 Eventually, at <u>Fort Laramie in 1851</u>, US government agent Thomas Fitzpatrick, met with the chiefs of the main Great Plains' tribes.

Treaty of Fort Laramie, 1851

The US government promised the chiefs:
• gifts
• an **annual payment of $50 000 for the next ten years** (although this was later reduced to five)
• that **each tribe would have its own reservation**, forbidden to whites.

In return, the Indian chiefs agreed to:
• **give up** the previously agreed **right of unlimited access** to the Great Plains
• **leave open the main routes** through Kansas and Nebraska.

2 However, the acceptance of <u>individual reservations divided and separated</u> the different tribes, and this <u>concentration policy</u> made it much easier for the US army <u>to control their movements</u>.

Chiefs did not have control over all their warriors, many of whom objected to the Treaty, which **restricted their traditional hunting and their right to roam across the Great Plains.**

Problems for the Native Americans

Of the two government bodies dealing with Native Americans, the **War Department** was more hostile than the **Indian Bureau. Most senior army officers** (Sherman, Sheridan, Custer, Chivington) **were extremely prejudiced** against Indians.

Many Indians soon resented the fact that, as well as being confined to reservations, they were **told to grow crops** (often on poor land) and **pressured to abandon their language and beliefs**.

Many of the **agents** who ran the reservations were **incompetent or even corrupt.** As a result, **food on the reservations was poor and often in short supply.**

PRACTICE

Study Source A below, and then answer the question which follows.

Source A Part of a report of 1853 by the Indian agent for the Upper Platte and Arkansas River Country, on the effect of wagon trains on the Oregon Trail on the life of the Plains Indians.

> They are in terrible want of food half the year. The travel upon the road [trail] drives the buffalo off or else confines them to a narrow path during the period of migration … their women are pinched with want and their children are constantly crying with hunger.

Use the provenance details, and your own knowledge, to explain your answer.

How reliable is Source A as historical evidence of the conditions experienced by Plains Indians on reservations set up after the Treaty of Fort Laramie, 1851?

THE AMERICAN WEST, 1840–1895

THE BARE BONES

> The increasing pressure from whites on the Great Plains led to more and more violent incidents.

> This led to the start of the Plains Wars in the 1860s.

> These wars continued, on and off, for the next 30 years. By 1890, the wars had ended, and the Plains Indians had lost their Great Plains.

A War for the South and Central Plains

KEY FACT

1 During the <u>1860s</u>, a series of conflicts broke out between the US army and the <u>Cheyenne and Arapaho in the Central Plains</u>, and the <u>Comanche and Kiowa in the Southern Plains</u>.

Remember
Over two-thirds of those killed at Sand Creek were women and children. Black Kettle managed to escape.

Disputes began to arise when, **in breach of the 1851 Fort Laramie Treaty**, large numbers of miners and settlers began **to move into Native American areas**.

In 1861, by the Treaty of Fort Lyon (aka Fort Wise), **Cheyenne and Arapaho** chiefs agreed to give up their 1851 reservations in return for **Sand Creek**, Colorado.

In September **1864**, their leader, **Black Kettle**, agreed with **Colonel J. M. Chivington** to return to Sand Creek. But, in October, Chivington attacked his camp, **massacring about 450 Indians**.

However, many Cheyenne warriors could not accept this. **During 1861–1864, they left the reservation** and carried out attacks on whites.

KEY FACT

2 This massacre outraged the <u>Cheyenne 'dog soldiers'</u>, and they began to <u>attack white settlements and wagon trains</u>.

Remember
The Indians' 'war to save the buffalo' ended in defeat. At the end of 1875, they agreed to return to their reservation.

This resulted in the **Red River War in 1874–1875**, the last outbreak of fighting on the Southern Plains, involving the **Kiowa** and the **Comanche**.

The war provoked by the Sand Creek massacre **forced the Plains tribes together**.

From the **early 1870s**, the US government supported the **wholesale slaughter of the buffalo** – the **Great Plains Massacre** – to **force the Indians to accept new terms**.

The path to escalating conflict

This war was finally **ended in 1867, by the Medicine Lodge Creek Treaty**. The Cheyenne and Arapaho were given **one shared reservation**, and the Comanche and Kiowa another.

Q What was the importance of the 'Great Plains Massacre' of the buffalo?

In November **1868, Custer** surprised a Cheyenne camp. In this **Battle of Washita**, over 100 Indians were killed, including Black Kettle. In January **1869**, a new agreement was signed at **Fort Cobb**.

But many **younger warriors** refused to accept the treaty and fighting broke out again in 1868. **Sherman and Sheridan** decided on a **winter campaign** against these Cheyenne.

THE AMERICAN WEST, 1840-1895

B   War for the North Plains

1   **The war on the Northern Plains involved the Sioux, and was <u>the last place of major resistance</u>.**

- Fighting in the **Northern Plains** broke out in **1862** over delayed annual payments and food distribution. It became known as **Little Crow's War**.

- More serious problems in the **mid-1860s** resulted from the **discovery of gold** in the remote North-West, which the US government wanted to develop.

- The government decided **in 1866 to build the Bozeman Trail**, even though this went right through the Sioux hunting grounds agreed in 1851.

- Little Crow's War and the Sand Creek Massacre made the Sioux determined to resist, leading to **Red Cloud's War, 1867–1868**. After some Sioux successes, this was ended by a second **Fort Laramie Treaty** at the end of **1868**.

- The US government agreed to stop work on the Bozeman Trail, and to 'give' **the whole of South Dakota as a Great Sioux Reservation**.

2   **However, <u>in 1874</u>, the US government ordered Custer <u>to survey the Black Hills, in South Dakota, for gold</u>.**

- The **discovery of gold** led to **thousands of miners pouring into the Black Hills**, in breach of the recent treaty.

- The Sioux **refused to sell their sacred land**, but mines and towns continued to spring up. Leadership passed to **Sitting Bull and Crazy Horse** who then led the **War for the Black Hills, 1875–1877**.

- Despite defeating Custer at the **Battle of the Little Bighorn in 1876**, the Sioux were eventually forced to return to their reservations.

3   **Life on the reservations was made even worse by <u>the Dawes (General Allotments) Act, 1887</u>.**

- This broke up much of the reservation land to create bigger farms of 160 acres, but **corrupt agents defrauded the Indians and sold the land to whites**.

- By **1890**, in desperation, many Sioux in South Dakota followed **Wovoka's Ghost Dance** idea.

- The authorities were alarmed as the Ghost Dance spread. However, the **Massacre at Wounded Knee, in December 1890**, ended the Ghost Dance and, effectively, the Plains Wars.

Remember (left margin)

Remember
By the time of the Dawes Act in 1887, Indian resistance was coming to an end. The Nez Perce had surrendered in 1877, and Geronimo, the Apache leader, in 1886.

Q How did the Dawes Act make life on the reservations more difficult?

PRACTICE

1 Why did the US government break the 1868 Fort Laramie Treaty?

2 Name the two Sioux leaders who defeated General Custer at the Battle of the Little Bighorn in 1876.

THE AMERICAN WEST, 1840–1895

Changes in Germany

THE BARE BONES

➤ By 1918, Germany was in a desperate state, on the verge of defeat and revolution.

➤ When the Kaiser (emperor) fled and abdicated, a new democratic provisional government agreed to sign an armistice with the Allies.

➤ In 1918–1919, revolutions broke out across Germany, but were eventually defeated.

A   Impact of the First World War

1 Most Germans believed they were fighting a defensive war. Right up to 1918, the Kaiser and the army High Command led people to believe that they were <u>winning the war</u>.

- However, the **Allied naval blockade** began to create serious shortages of food and medicines in Germany. The food problems were made worse by the 1916–1917 winter and the loss of the potato crop.

- This forced German civilians to rely on turnips instead in what was called the **'turnip winter'**.

- By 1917, these shortages began to affect Germany's armed forces – cuts in navy rations led to a mutiny.

- Coal shortages then led to electricity cuts. By early 1918, many Germans were fed up with the war. Then an **influenza epidemic** hit, killing many civilians and soldiers.

2 In October 1918, the German army was <u>near defeat</u>. So the High Command told the Kaiser that Germany could not win the war, and advised him to <u>seek peace terms</u>.

- However, the USA told the Kaiser that there was no possibility of peace negotiations **until Germany became more democratic**.

- By then, the Allied naval blockade was creating **near-starvation** conditions and Germany was in financial ruin.

- Despite this, **the Kaiser refused to give more power** to the German Reichstag (parliament).

- Knowledge of the desperate situation of the German army was kept from the public. Because no Allied troops had reached German territory, Germans still believed Germany was winning the war.

- So most Germans were shocked when later, in November 1918, an armistice was signed, because they did not know that the army was collapsing.

KEY FACT

Remember
Germany had never been a full democracy under the Kaiser. The powers of parliament had been limited, and free speech was restricted.

KEY FACT

Q Why was the winter of 1916–1917 known as the 'turnip winter' in Germany?

GERMANY, 1918–1945

B Revolution

1 On 28 October 1918, angry sailors at the <u>Kiel naval base</u> mutinied. Unlike the 1917 mutiny, this one <u>spread quickly</u>.

The sailors were soon joined by soldiers and workers. Imitating the November 1917 revolution in Russia, many began to form **workers' and soldiers' soviets (councils).**

In a matter of days, revolutionaries took control of several towns. In **Bavaria and Saxony**, socialists declared their provinces to be independent republics.

As the mutinies and uprisings spread across Germany, the Kaiser still refused to share power with the Reichstag.

2 By 9 November, Berlin was in the hands of the revolutionaries; on 10 November, <u>the Kaiser abdicated</u>.

A **centre-left coalition provisional government** was then set up under the leadership of Ebert of the Social Democratic Party (SPD). He declared Germany a **democratic republic**.

The army generals told the new provisional government that the army could no longer fight so it had no choice but to agree to **sign an armistice** with the Allies on 11 November.

The new government then arranged for elections in January 1919.

3 However, in Berlin in December, the revolutionary socialists of the <u>Spartacist League</u> tried to start a workers' revolution similar to the Russian one in November 1917.

Ebert, under pressure from army leaders, agreed to call in the army to crush this **Spartacist Revolt**.

Noske, the SPD Defence Minister, also used a paramilitary group of unemployed right-wing nationalist soldiers (**the Freikorps**) to put down the rising.

The Freikorps were not just anti-Communist and anti-socialist – they also hated democracy. Thousands of workers were killed during the suppression, including the leaders, **Karl Liebknecht and Rosa Luxemburg**, who were captured and then murdered.

1 Why were most Germans surprised when an armistice was signed in November 1918?

2 Why did the Spartacists attempt a revolution in the winter of 1918–1919?

GERMANY, 1918–1945

Weimar Germany, 1919-1923

THE BARE BONES

➤ A new constitution (known as the Weimar Constitution) gave the German people full democracy for the first time.

➤ The new Weimar Republic faced many problems in this period, in addition to the opposition of those who supported the Kaiser and who hated the Treaty of Versailles.

➤ There was much violent political opposition to the Weimar Republic, from the right and the left.

➤ There were also serious economic problems, connected to the war and reparations.

A Establishment of the Weimar Republic

KEY FACT

1 Germany from 1919 to 1933 is usually referred to as the Weimar Republic or Weimar Germany. This is because the Spartacist Revolt of 1919 and its suppression in Berlin forced the provisional government to move to Weimar to draw up a new democratic constitution for Germany.

Remember
The Fundamental Rights section of the constitution guaranteed freedom of speech, religious belief and travel.

- The new Weimar Constitution gave the vote to all people over 20 years of age. It used a system of **proportional representation (PR)** for elections to the **Reichstag**.

- Elections were to take place every four years. Governments – headed by a Chancellor (Prime Minister) – were to be chosen from, and responsible to, the Reichstag.

- Germany became a federal system, with power shared between central government and **18 new Länder (state) governments**.

KEY FACT

2 Article 48 of the constitution gave the President emergency powers to rule by decree without the Reichstag, and even to suspend the constitution. The President was to be directly elected, every seven years.

- Due to the system of PR, there were many small parties in the Reichstag. This meant that most Weimar governments were often short-lived **coalitions**. From 1919–1923, Germany had nine coalition governments – these often found it difficult to agree on policies.

Q Which two main powers did Article 48 of the Weimar Constitution give to the President?

- Many Germans were bitterly angry at the Treaty of Versailles. They blamed the new government for signing it, and referred to them as the **November Criminals** who had 'stabbed Germany in the back'.

GERMANY, 1918-1945

B Early problems

1 Many Germans hated the new government for signing the armistice and the Treaty of Versailles. They were opposed to democracy and <u>preferred the authoritarian rule of the Kaiser. They saw democracy as a foreign idea imposed on Germany by the Allies.</u>

KEY FACT

Remember
Most of the civil servants, judges, and army and police officers who had served under the Kaiser kept their jobs after 1918, but many were opposed to the democracy of the Weimar Constitution.

LEFT		RIGHT
• The new **Communist Party (KPD)** organised strikes and another attempt at revolution in Berlin in March 1919. As in January, these were suppressed by the army and the Freikorps. • There was also an unsuccessful Communist uprising in Munich in which the army shot many workers. • A **Communist uprising in the Ruhr** following Kapp's Putsch of 1920 was suppressed by the army and Freikorps, who shot over 2000 workers.	**Opposition to the Weimar Republic**	• **Extreme nationalist groups** carried out numerous murders of left-wing and liberal politicians between 1920 and 1923. • In March 1920, the army made no effort to stop **Kapp's Putsch** – an attempted Freikorps coup against the government. It was defeated by a general strike organised by Berlin's workers.

KEY FACT

2 There were also <u>serious economic problems</u> after the war, which brought the German economy near to collapse by 1920.

In 1922, Germany said it could not afford to pay its second reparations instalment.

So, **in 1923, French and Belgian troops occupied the Ruhr**, Germany's richest industrial area, in order to take food, coal, iron ore and steel as payment. This was done without Britain's support.

Germany replied with **'passive resistance'** (strikes and non-co-operation). The French deported 150 000 strikers and 132 Germans were killed in separate incidents.

The German economy collapsed, leading to **hyper-inflation** (massive and rapid price increases), which even began to affect France.

A new German government, led by **Stresemann**, ended passive resistance, and the French finally withdrew.

Q What action did the German army take against Kapp's Putsch in 1920?

PRACTICE

1 Why did France and Belgium occupy the Ruhr in January 1923?

2 What was the hyper-inflation of 1923?

GERMANY, 1918–1945

THE BARE BONES

➤ In 1920, a new right-wing party – the Nazi Party – was set up. In 1921, Adolf Hitler became its new leader.

➤ In 1923, this party made an unsuccessful attempt to overthrow the government in Munich.

A The origins and beliefs of the Nazi Party

KEY FACT

1 In 1920, <u>the NSDAP (Nazi Party)</u> was formed and, in 1921, <u>Adolf Hitler</u> became its leader.

- **Hitler, an Austrian born in 1889, had moved to Germany** to avoid military service in the Austro-Hungarian army.

- When the First World War broke out in 1914, he joined the German army. Like many, he was shocked to hear that Germany had surrendered in 1918.

Q What job did the German army give Hitler after the war?

- After the bloody suppression of the socialist revolution in Bavaria, in March 1919 he worked for the German army as a political instructor whose task was **to indoctrinate new recruits against socialist and democratic ideas**.

KEY FACT

2 Hitler was then sent by the army to Munich to spy on the small <u>German Workers' Party (DAP)</u>, which they thought might be a left-wing party.

- In fact, DAP was an extreme right-wing nationalist party, led by **Anton Drexler**, who was violently anti-Communist and anti-semitic (anti-Jewish).

Remember
Anti-semitism means hatred of Jewish people. It had existed in Europe for centuries, and mostly involved discrimination in employment and housing, although violent 'pogroms' had taken place in Tsarist Russia and Poland.

- Reassured, the army decided DAP would be useful for spreading nationalist ideas and so gave it money.

- After attending and speaking at a few of the party's meetings, **Hitler decided to join**.

- In **1920**, he persuaded it to change its name to the **National Socialist German Workers' Party (NSDAP)**. It soon became known as the **Nazi Party**.

- Hitler helped design an emblem for the party based on the **swastika** – it was black (for the 'Aryan' struggle against Jews) on a white circle (for nationalism) with a red background (for the workers).

- In 1920, Hitler persuaded the new party to adopt a **25-point programme** that he had helped to write.

Q When did Hitler become leader of the Nazi Party?

- The programme contained mainly **nationalist and anti-semitic policies**, with some vague 'socialist' elements (such as better pensions).

GERMANY, 1918-1945

B Nazi Party actions

1 In 1921, Hitler replaced Drexler as party leader.

STEPS IN THE RISE OF THE NAZIS

By 1923, the Nazis had over **50 000 members in southern Germany**, and received donations from various sources, including the army.

The SA soon came under the leadership of **Ernst Rohm**, a local army captain. He helped the Nazis get **funds from the army** to buy up the *Volkischer Beobachter*, a local weekly newspaper.

Hitler set up the **Stormtroopers (SA)**. These **'Brownshirts'** (so called because of their uniform) were mainly unemployed ex-soldiers who attacked left-wing political meetings and demonstrations.

2 When the German government called off passive resistance against the French occupation of the Ruhr in September 1923, German nationalists were furious.

- In November, Hitler decided to march to Berlin from Munich (where the Nazis were strongest) to overthrow the Weimar government in a **'National Revolution'** (usually known as the **Beer Hall, or Munich, Putsch**).

- The Nazis took over a **beer hall meeting** that was being addressed by **important Bavarian officials**.

- At first, Hitler persuaded them to support his **'March on Berlin'**. Although they later withdrew, Hitler went ahead with his plans, supported by **Hermann Goring and General Ludendorff** (a First World War leader).

- The march by **3000 SA** members was stopped by armed police. In the fighting that followed, one policeman and 16 Nazis were killed. Hitler ran away, but was later found hiding in an attic and was arrested.

- He was **accused of treason**, but the Munich judge allowed him to make long speeches at this trial, which were **widely reported** by sympathetic newspapers.

- In April 1924, Hitler was given the lightest possible sentence – five years in **Landsberg Prison** (the maximum was life).

Study Source A, and then answer the question which follows.

Source A
Nazi Stormtroopers arresting the Mayor of Munich, 9 November 1923.

What does Source A tell us about the Beer Hall Putsch of 1923? Use the source, and your own knowledge, to explain your answer.

GERMANY, 1918–1945

THE BARE BONES

➤ The 1923 hyper-inflation in Germany caused great hardship.

➤ In September 1923, Gustav Stresemann became Chancellor. Under him, Germany prospered in the 'Golden Years'.

➤ Stresemann's economic and diplomatic achievements meant more extreme parties did badly in elections. For the Nazi Party, the years 1924–1929 became known as the 'Lean Years'.

A Stresemann and the 'Golden Years'

1 By the time Stresemann became Chancellor in September 1923, many Germans were suffering greatly from the effects of <u>hyper-inflation</u>.

Remember
Stresemann's diplomatic agreements led to greater foreign investment in Germany as international relations improved.

Q What did the Dawes Plan and the Young Plan do about Germany's reparation payments?

Money had become so worthless that workers had to be paid twice a day so items could be bought before prices went up again.

Stresemann called off passive resistance, and **promised to pay reparations**.

In **1924**, Stresemann negotiated the **Dawes Plan** with the USA. This **reduced the size of reparation instalments**, and provided Germany with **US loans** that were used to modernise factories and build new ones.

German industry began to revive and unemployment fell. Stresemann then began to restore Germany's position by co-operating with the Allies.

In November 1923, Stresemann introduced a **new currency (the Rentenmark)** to end inflation.

In **1929**, the **Young Plan** brought **more loans**, while **reparations were reduced and spread over 60 years**.

Between 1924 and 1929, Germany received over 25 billion gold marks in loans – three times more than reparation payments. By 1929, Germany was second only to the USA in advanced industrial production.

2 Stresemann, who went from being Chancellor to Foreign Minister, also <u>improved Germany's diplomatic position</u>.

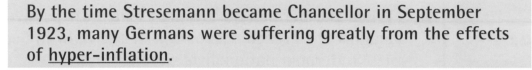

Germany joins the League of Nations, 1926.

Stresemann's diplomacy

Kellogg-Briand Pact, 1928 – Germany, along with 44 other countries, renounced war.

Locarno Treaty, 1925 – accepted Germany's 1919 western frontiers, and said changes in the east would only be by negotiation.

B   The Nazis' 'Lean Years'

1   During the period 1924–1929, Stresemann's policies achieved some of the changes demanded by the right.

- As a result, **support for extreme parties declined.**
- Although Hitler had been sentenced to five years for his part in the **Beer Hall Putsch,** he was released in December 1924 after serving only nine months.

2   While Hitler was in prison, he wrote *Mein Kampf* (*My Struggle*). When he was released, he found Germany much improved and the Nazi Party banned, split into factions, and suffering from a fall-off in membership.

- As a result, the Nazis did badly in elections in the period 1924–1930 – this period is known as **the Nazis' 'Lean Years'.**
- Hitler reorganised the party. It was relaunched in 1925, and power was concentrated in Hitler's hands. Special sections (for students, teachers, farmers, and the Hitler Youth for young people) were set up to recruit more members. Party branches were set up all over Germany.
- **In 1926, Joseph Goebbels took control of Nazi Party propaganda.** By 1928, the Nazis had just over 10 000 members.

3   Hitler also decided that to win power the Nazis would have to use elections.

- The experience of the Beer Hall Putsch convinced him of the **need to win over the army and wealthy industrialists.**
- However, Hitler had no intentions of abandoning violence – in 1925, he set up the **black-shirted SS (Schutz Staffel).**
- Officially, this was his personal bodyguard, but it soon increased in size and attacked opponents. **In 1929, Heinrich Himmler became its head.**

Study Source A below, and then answer the questions which follow.

Source A An extract from a letter by Hitler written in 1923 while he was in prison in Landsberg Castle.

1 Why, by 1923, did Hitler think that he had to change his tactics for gaining power?

2 How did he reorganise the Nazi Party in the years 1925–1929?

When I resume active work it will be necessary to pursue a new policy. Instead of working to achieve power by an armed coup, we will have to hold our noses and enter the Reichstag against the Catholic and Marxist members. If outvoting them takes longer than outshooting them, at least the result will be guaranteed by their own constitution. Any lawful process is slow. Sooner or later we will have a majority, and after that – Germany!

GERMANY, 1918–1945

The Nazis come to power

➤ The Great Depression, which began in 1929, soon affected Germany badly.

➤ As coalition governments fell, President Paul von Hindenburg increasingly ruled by decree.

➤ The Nazis gained popular support and, by 1932, were the largest single party. In January 1933, Hitler became Chancellor.

A The impact of the Depression

KEY FACT

Remember
Population increase meant that unemployment never dropped below 1.25 million.

1 In 1929, the German economy seemed to be booming, but it was <u>not as strong as it appeared</u>.

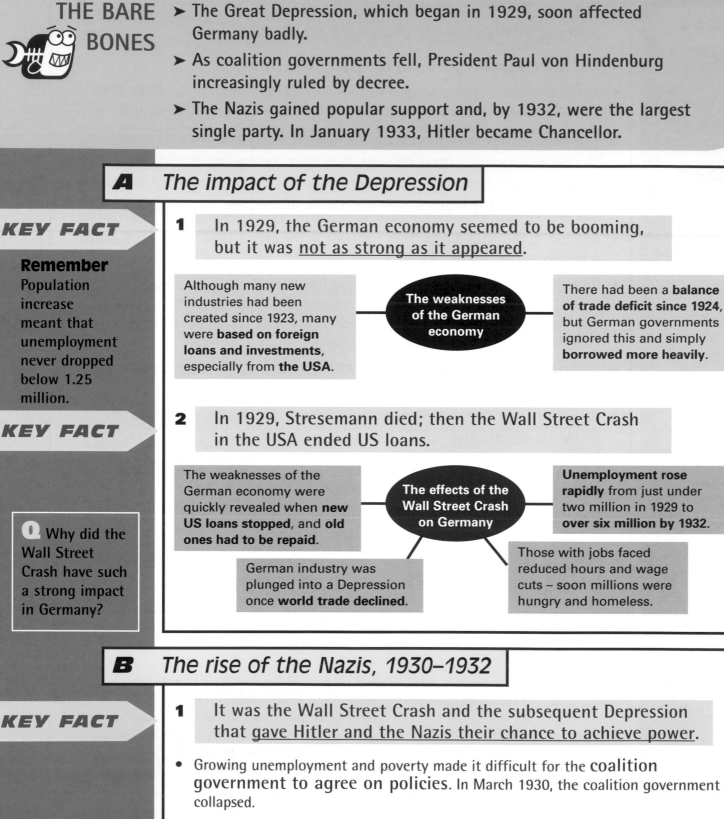

Although many new industries had been created since 1923, many were **based on foreign loans and investments**, especially from **the USA**.

The weaknesses of the German economy

There had been a **balance of trade deficit since 1924**, but German governments ignored this and simply **borrowed more heavily**.

KEY FACT

2 In 1929, Stresemann died; then the Wall Street Crash in the USA ended US loans.

Q Why did the Wall Street Crash have such a strong impact in Germany?

The weaknesses of the German economy were quickly revealed when **new US loans stopped**, and **old ones had to be repaid**.

The effects of the Wall Street Crash on Germany

Unemployment rose rapidly from just under two million in 1929 to **over six million by 1932**.

German industry was plunged into a Depression once **world trade declined**.

Those with jobs faced reduced hours and wage cuts – soon millions were hungry and homeless.

B The rise of the Nazis, 1930–1932

KEY FACT

1 It was the Wall Street Crash and the subsequent Depression that <u>gave Hitler and the Nazis their chance to achieve power</u>.

• Growing unemployment and poverty made it difficult for the **coalition government to agree on policies**. In March 1930, the coalition government collapsed.

• **President Hindenburg** (elected in 1925) appointed Heinrich Bruning, from the Centre Party, as Chancellor.

GERMANY, 1918-1945

B

2 Political confusion and economic crisis led many conservative Germans to turn to extreme right-wing parties.

- In September 1930, the Nazis increased their share from 12 to 107 seats.

- At the same time, more and more workers began to support the KPD. In 1930, they won 77 seats.

- When governments failed to get majority support in the Reichstag, Hindenburg increasingly ruled by decree. By 1932, over 15 million Germans were dependent on state benefits or charity.

3 The growth of the Communists worried <u>wealthy industrialists</u> – <u>they began to give funds to the Nazis</u>.

- These funds financed massive propaganda in the 1932 elections, masterminded by Goebbels.

- In the April presidential election, Hitler won 13 million votes compared to Hindenburg's 19 million; in the July elections, the Nazis became the biggest party with 230 seats.

4 The Nazi rise was also helped by the <u>violence of the SA</u>, which numbered about 500 000 in 1932.

- In the November 1932 elections, the Nazis remained the largest party but lost 34 seats. The Communists rose again to 100 seats.

- In December, Hindenburg replaced Franz von Papen with General Kurt von Schleicher. But political rivalries soon led to the collapse of this government.

- In January 1933, von Papen (leader of the Nationalists) persuaded Hindenburg to appoint Hitler as Chancellor of a nationalist/conservative-dominated coalition.

Why did ealthy dustrialists ve large onations to e Nazi Party efore 1930?

PRACTICE

Study Source A, and then answer the questions which follow.

Source A A table showing the number of seats won by parties in elections to the Reichstag, 1928–1932.

	1928	1930	1932 July	1932 Nov
Nazis	12	107	230	196
German Nationalist Party (DNVP)	73	41	37	52
German People's Party (DVP)	45	30	7	11
Centre Party	62	68	75	70
German Democratic Party (DDP)	25	20	4	2
Social Democratic Party (SPD)	153	143	133	121
Communists	54	77	89	100
Other	67	91	33	32
Total	**491**	**577**	**608**	**584**

1 Which three parties, according to this source, tended to dominate elections in Weimar Germany during the period 1928–1932?

2 What do these election results tell us about politics in Weimar Germany?

GERMANY, 1918–1945

The Nazi dictatorship

THE BARE BONES

➤ After Hitler became Chancellor, he moved quickly to establish a Nazi dictatorship, often using the legal procedures of the Weimar constitution. By 1934, Germany was under Nazi control.

➤ Once established, the Nazi dictatorship was maintained in several ways, including a constant campaign of terror and propaganda.

A Establishing the Nazi dictatorship

KEY FACT

1 Although there were only three Nazi ministers in Hitler's government, he planned to take complete power.

- Hitler called a new election for March 1933, and SA and SS violence increased.

- In February, just before the elections, the **Reichstag fire** took place – the Nazis blamed the Communists, whose leaders and candidates were quickly rounded up.

- In Prussia (the largest Länd or state), the Minister of the Interior was **Goring**, a leading Nazi. He enrolled SA members into the police – over 4000 KPD and SPD members were arrested, their meetings broken up and their newspapers banned.

- The Nazis failed to get an overall majority in the Reichstag, despite banning those Communists who had managed to get elected. **The Nationalists then agreed to support the Nazis – this gave Hitler control.**

KEY FACT

2 By intimidating or excluding SPD deputies, Hitler got the Reichstag to pass the <u>Enabling Act in March 1933</u>.

Q Why was the Enabling Act so crucial to Hitler's plan to destroy the Republic?

- Hindenburg agreed to suspend the constitution and gave Hitler **power to rule by decree for four years**. Hitler then quickly destroyed Weimar democracy.

- In April, all 18 Länder were taken over by Nazi gauleiters (regional party officials). In May, **trade unions were banned**, and in July **all opposition parties were banned (or persuaded to disband)** and **Germany became a one-party dictatorship**. By then, most KPD and SPD leaders and activists were in **concentration camps run by the SA**.

KEY FACT

3 Hitler also faced opposition from the more militant wing of the SA, including its leader <u>Ernst Rohm</u>.

Remember
Militants in the SA also wanted Hitler to carry out the left-wing promises of the Party Programme.

- Among other demands, the SA wanted to become the new German army. The army officers and the industrialists opposed Rohm's plans.

- **In June 1934, Hitler ordered the Night of the Long Knives,** in which the SS (with army help) murdered Rohm and other SA leaders.

- This reassured the generals and, when Hindenburg died in August, **they supported Hitler becoming Führer of Germany** – Hitler was now President, Chancellor and Commander-in-Chief of the armed forces.

B Terror and propaganda

1 The terror campaign was carried out by <u>the Gestapo</u> (secret police) and <u>the SS</u> (which, by 1935, had risen to over 200 000). <u>Both were controlled by Himmler.</u>

Informers

About 400 000 'Block Leaders'

Methods of Nazi terror

Mass arrests to intimidate potential opponents

Concentration camps – the SS took them over in 1934 and by 1939, there were six.

2 The Nazis also made skilful use of censorship and propaganda to isolate opponents and build support. This was directed by <u>Goebbels as Minister of Propaganda and Culture.</u>

Cheap radios were produced.

The Nazis' massive **Nuremberg rallies** were filmed for the cinema, which also reflected Nazi ideology.

Nazi censorship and propaganda

Loudspeakers were placed in all workplaces and public areas to ensure everyone heard Nazi views.

Works of literature and art that conflicted with Nazi ideas were outlawed and destroyed.

Newspapers were banned or censored.

KEY FACT

Remember At first, concentration camps were mainly for political prisoners.

KEY FACT

Q How did Goebbels try to indoctrinate the German people after 1933?

PRACTICE

Study Source A below, and then answer the question which follows.

Source A Communists arrested by the SA in Berlin, shortly after Hitler had become Chancellor in 1933.

Try to give several different reasons in your answer, not just one.

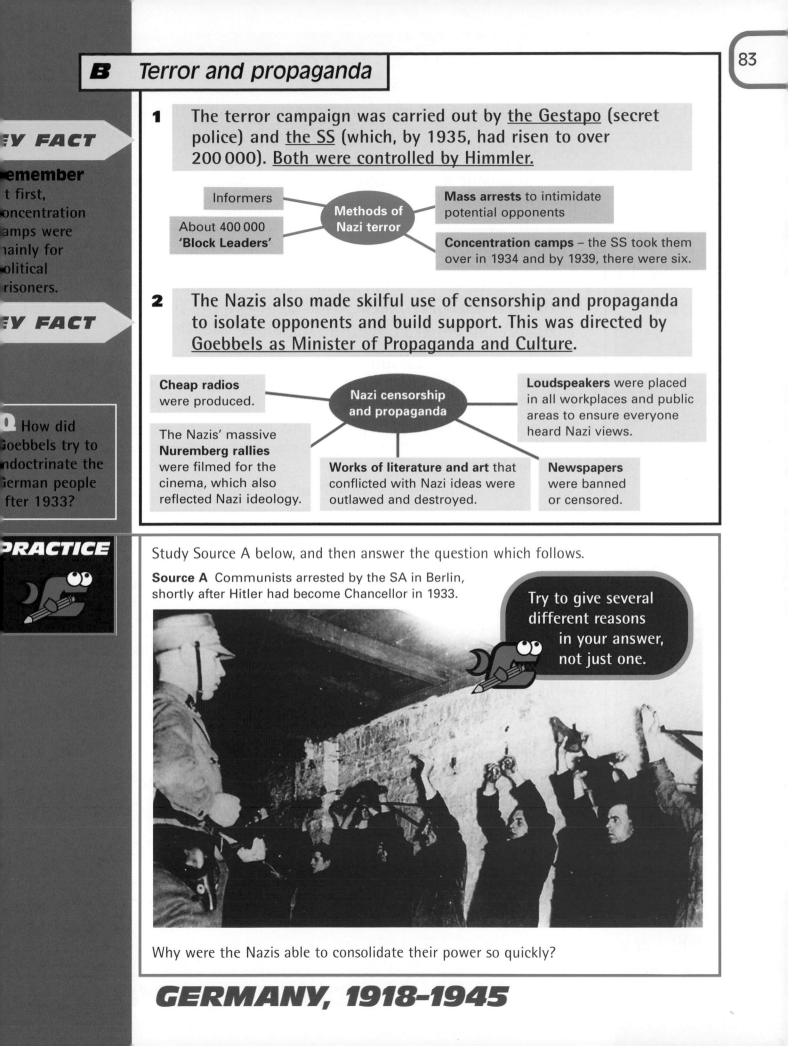

Why were the Nazis able to consolidate their power so quickly?

GERMANY, 1918–1945

Nazi economic policy

THE BARE BONES

➤ Nazi control was not just maintained by a combination of terror and propaganda. It was also assisted by the adoption of popular economic policies.

➤ These economic policies were to do with reducing unemployment, promoting self-sufficiency, and German rearmament.

A Unemployment

KEY FACT

1 Despite the earlier promises of their 25-point programme, the new Nazi government made <u>no attempt to limit the wealth and power of big firms</u>, let alone take them over.

Remember
Communists, Jews, women forced out of jobs, and those in concentration camps, were not counted as unemployed.

• Instead, Hitler tried to **reassure big business** by keeping **Hjalmar Schacht** as **head of the Reichsbank**, and then making him **Minister of the Economy**.

• In order to achieve his **foreign policy aims**, Hitler knew he needed to reduce unemployment and strengthen the German economy so that Germany could rearm and be self-sufficient.

• Schacht's role was to develop a **'New Plan'** which, in part, was to find a way to finance public works and so reduce unemployment without increasing Germany's foreign debts.

• The Nazis dealt with **unemployment** in several ways.

The National Labour Service (Arbeitdienst), set up before 1933, was expanded. In **1935**, the **Reich Labour Law** made it compulsory for all men aged 18–25 for six months.

Nazi strategies against unemployment

Public works funded by government money gave work to the unemployed. The main projects were building houses, hospitals, schools and, especially roads (to allow quick movement of troops) and barracks.

• By 1939, unemployment had officially fallen to 100 000.

KEY FACT

2 Although this pleased many workers, other Nazi policies were less popular, as they resulted in <u>real wages</u> remaining <u>below the levels of 1929</u>, despite the introduction of food price controls.

Q Why were many workers disappointed with Nazi policies after 1933?

• When trade unions were abolished in 1933, all workers had to join the Nazis' **German Labour Front (DAF)**. Strikes were made illegal, wages remained low even after full employment, and the hours of work rose.

A

- To distract from this, the DAF organised two schemes: the **'Beauty of Labour (SDA)'** to improve working conditions (though little was achieved) and the **'Strength Through Joy (KfD)'** to provide cheap holidays and leisure activities.
- However, the KfD's **Volkswagen (people's car) scheme** tricked workers into paying five marks a week into a fund to buy one. But the few which were eventually produced went to Nazi officials, and most of the money was used for rearmament.

B   *Self-sufficiency and rearmament*

1   Under Schacht, agricultural production was increased, imports were reduced, and attempts were made to find substitutes for foreign goods so that Germany could become <u>self-sufficient</u>.

- Self-sufficiency would **cut Germany's import bills** and give Germany the **raw materials** needed for rearmament. It was therefore closely connected to Hitler's **war aims**. The search for **substitute products** also helped reduce unemployment.
- As well as trying to **increase agricultural production**, the Nazis tried to keep food prices below the levels of 1928–1929.
- This disappointed many **small farmers** who had strongly supported the Nazis in the 1920s and early 1930s. Although the **Reich Entailed Farm Law, 1933**, gave farmers some protection from eviction because of debt, it also prevented small peasant farmers from splitting up their farms between their sons.

2   <u>Rearmament</u> began in 1933 in secret but, by 1935, was carried out openly.

- Rearmament gave employment to many, as did the **re-introduction of conscription**, which increased the army to **1.4 million** (although previous governments had already begun to increase it).
- In 1936, **Goring** was ordered to get Germany ready for war, by preparing a **Four-Year Plan**.
- However, Goring's Four-Year Plan, with its growing demand for resources, **undermined Schacht's work**.
- Hitler refused to slow down the rearmament programme so, **in 1937, Schacht resigned**.

Q What was
he purpose of
he Four-Year
Plan of 1936?

1 Identify two ways in which the Nazis tried to reduce unemployment after 1933.

2 Why did Schacht resign as Minister of the Economy in 1937?

GERMANY, 1918-1945

THE BARE BONES

➤ The Nazis introduced various social policies to maintain their control of Germany, and create a national 'people's (or 'folk') community' – a 'Volksgemeinschaft'.

➤ The roles of women and young people were particularly important in the creation of this community.

A   Women

KEY FACT

1 The Nazis tried to control <u>women and their role</u>, to make sure they played a part in creating an <u>'Aryan'</u> society. Nazi policies for women were based on the <u>'3 Ks' (Kinder, Kirche, Kuche)</u>.

- The Nazis believed in the **'natural' division between the genders**. They believed men were 'born' to work, engage in politics and fight wars while women were 'intended by nature' to be **passive housewives and mothers**.

- If women did work outside the home, the Nazis believed their work should be related to their **'natural' roles**, such as cleaning, cooking, nursing or social work.

KEY FACT

2 To make sure women conformed to their <u>roles in the Nazi Third Reich</u>, a range of different policies was introduced.

Remember
The Nazis even tried to control women's appearance so that it conformed to 'traditional' images.

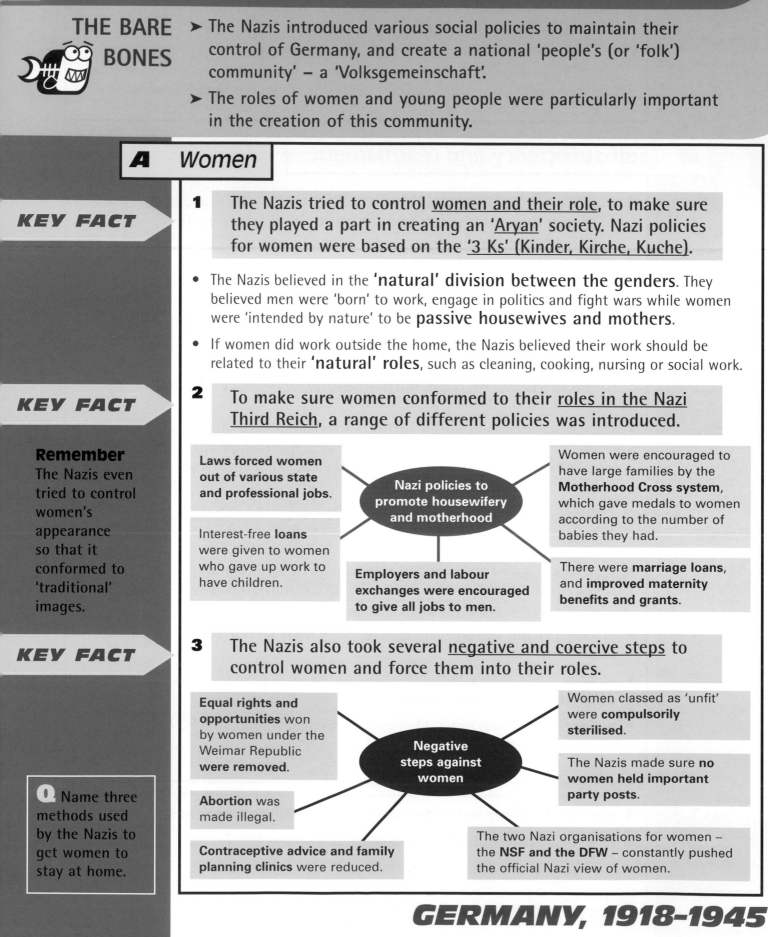

Laws forced women out of various state and professional jobs.

Nazi policies to promote housewifery and motherhood

Women were encouraged to have large families by the **Motherhood Cross system**, which gave medals to women according to the number of babies they had.

Interest-free **loans** were given to women who gave up work to have children.

Employers and labour exchanges were encouraged to give all jobs to men.

There were **marriage loans**, and **improved maternity benefits and grants**.

KEY FACT

3 The Nazis also took several <u>negative and coercive steps</u> to control women and force them into their roles.

Equal rights and opportunities won by women under the Weimar Republic **were removed**.

Women classed as 'unfit' were **compulsorily sterilised**.

Negative steps against women

The Nazis made sure **no women held important party posts**.

Abortion was made illegal.

Q Name three methods used by the Nazis to get women to stay at home.

Contraceptive advice and family planning clinics were reduced.

The two Nazi organisations for women – the **NSF and the DFW** – constantly pushed the official Nazi view of women.

B Young people

Y FACT

Q Which three chool subjects id the Nazis mphasise in heir new urriculum?

Remember
ll 'unreliable' nti-Nazi or ewish) teachers ere sacked.

Y FACT

Remember
lthough embership of ne Hitler Youth as eventually ade ompulsory, ecent evidence uggests that any children till did not join.

---

1 The Nazis wanted to control <u>young people</u> to ensure they filled their <u>'proper' adult roles</u>, and gave <u>support</u> to the Nazis in the future.

To make sure all children received the 'right' ideas, **all politically and racially 'unreliable' teachers were sacked.**

All teachers had to swear loyalty to Hitler and join the **Nazis' Teachers' League.**

A new **national curriculum** was drawn up and centrally imposed, with all schools coming under government control. In **1934, Bernhard Rust** became Minister for Science and Education.

Nazi control in schools

Great emphasis was placed on **history** in order to show the 'greatness' of the Nazis. Great emphasis was placed on **biology** in order to teach 'race science' that stressed the superiority of Aryans.

The amount of time dedicated to **PE** was tripled in order to get boys fit for the army and girls fit to be mothers. Any child with any **physical handicap** was prevented from receiving secondary education.

In history, **all textbooks were replaced by one official one**, which attacked the 'enemies' of Germany, and showed how the Nazis were 'saving' Germany.

- One result of these changes was a **decline in educational standards**.

2 Out of school, young people were encouraged to join the Nazis' <u>Hitler Youth</u> movements. There were separate ones for boys and girls, and for different age groups.

- In July 1933, **Baldur von Schirach**, the leader of the Hitler Youth, became **Youth Leader of the Reich**. There was often rivalry between him and Rust.
- All members attended **Hitler Youth camps** every year.
- There were special schools for those members who got the best marks – **Adolf Hitler Schools** and **Order Castles**.
- The emphasis was on **keeping fit**, and on **training for male and female roles in adult life** – war for boys and motherhood for girls.
- In 1936, **the Hitler Youth Law** made the Hitler Youth officially as important as school and the family, and so increased pressure on parents to make sure their children joined.
- In 1939, **membership of the Hitler Youth became compulsory.**

PRACTICE

1 How did the lives of women change under the Nazis?

2 Why were the Nazis so concerned to control young people?

GERMANY, 1918-1945

Outside the Nazi 'community'

THE BARE BONES

➤ While many people supported Nazi policies, there were also those who remained excluded from the Nazis' Volksgemeinschaft.

➤ Jews were particularly excluded from this 'community'. After 1933, Nazi policies against the Jews became increasingly violent.

A Early policies, 1933–1938

KEY FACT

Remember
The Nazis' racial ideas also led to euthanasia of the disabled and compulsory sterilisation.

1 The Nazis were deeply racist and believed the '<u>Aryan race</u>' (the blue-eyed, blond, North European people) '<u>created culture</u>' and were therefore <u>superior to all other races</u>.

- All non-Aryan groups were **inferior** – the **'subhuman' (Untermenschen)** Jews, Blacks, Slavs and gypsies (Sinti and Roma) were seen as 'destroyers of culture'.

- The Nazis wanted to create a pure 'Aryan master race' **(Ubermenschen or Herrenvolk).** Only 'Aryans' could belong to the Volksgemeinschaft.

KEY FACT

Remember
In 1938, all Jewish men and women had to add 'Israel' or 'Sarah' to their names and have their passports stamped with the letter 'J'.

2 The main victims of Nazi racism were <u>Jewish people</u>, even though there were only about 550 000 Jewish people in Germany (about one per cent of the population).

After Hitler became Chancellor in January 1933, the amount of **Nazi propaganda against Jews** was **increased**.

In April 1933, Hitler ordered the SA and SS to organise a **boycott of Jewish shops**.

Hitler decided to use the law to attack Jews. **Laws were passed to sack Jews from the civil service, the law and education.**

Persecution of the Jews

In 1935, the Nuremberg Laws were passed. These removed German citizenship from all Jews and forbade inter-marriage.

In 1934, Jews were **banned from public facilities such as parks and swimming pools**.

KEY FACT

3 After 1936, other laws further <u>restricted the rights of Jews to work or own property</u>, and <u>forced all Jewish children out of state schools</u>.

- In November 1938, Kristallnacht (Night of Broken Glass) saw attacks on Jews by the SS and SA (encouraged by Goebbels).

- About 100 Jews were killed, over 20 000 were put in concentration camps, and thousands of homes and shops were destroyed.

- After a week of terror, the Nazis fined the Jews one billion marks. By **1939**, nearly all Jewish businesses had been **forced to close down or sell up**.

GERMANY, 1918–1945

B The Holocaust

1

After the Second World War began in 1939, Nazi actions became even more extreme. As Nazi Germany conquered more and more countries, the number of Jews coming under Nazi rule greatly increased.

All Jews in Poland, and the countries of Northern and Western Europe invaded by the Nazis during 1939–1940, **were forced to live in ghettos**.

The inhabitants of these ghettos were **deprived of food and medical supplies** deliberately, and were made to work in **forced labour camps**.

After the invasion of the USSR in **June 1941**, another **five million** Jews came under Nazi control.

2

At first, the Nazi leaders considered various 'options' for dealing with the Jews of Europe. These included the 'Madagascar Plan' (forcible deportation), slave labour camps and mass extermination.

In July 1941, **Goring** sent a written order to **Reinhard Heydrich** to prepare the **'Final Solution of the Jewish Question'**. In the summer of 1941, **Himmler ordered the SS to form 'Special Action'** groups to kill all Soviet Jews.

At the **Wannsee Conference, January 1942**, leading Nazis decided to exterminate all Jews in Europe, with **Adolf Eichmann** in charge of overall planning.

Extermination camps using gas chambers and ovens (for example, Auschwitz) were built in Eastern Europe. About **six million** Jews died in this **Holocaust**.

PRACTICE

Study Source A below and then answer the question which follows.

Source A Jewish women and children being taken from their homes to an extermination camp.

GERMANY, 1918–1945

Opposition

THE BARE BONES

➤ Although many Germans supported Hitler, especially before 1939, there were also Nazi opponents, some of whom continued to resist after 1933, despite the risks.

➤ There was opposition from political groups, from young people, and from religious groups and individuals.

➤ After the outbreak of the Second World War, opposition from sections of the German elites also began to grow.

A Politicals and young people

KEY FACT

1 In March 1933, the Nazis had won only 43 per cent of the vote despite intimidation and violence. There were many 'politicals' who continued to oppose Hitler's regime after 1933, even though most of them lost their lives doing so.

Remember
Many Germans supported Nazi policies on unemployment, rearmament and foreign expansion.

• **The Communists (KPD) and the Social Democrats (SPD)** set up underground organisations. Although they still refused to co-operate, both groups **published anti-Nazi leaflets** and **organised industrial sabotage and strikes**.

• The Communist **Red Orchestra (Rote Kapelle)** group also passed on **military secrets** to the Soviet Union until its members were eventually betrayed to the Gestapo.

KEY FACT

2 There was opposition from thousands of <u>young people</u> to Nazi ideas and actions.

• Some young people organised political opposition – the most famous were the **White Rose Group**.

• This group was set up by **university students in Munich**. They **distributed leaflets, wrote anti-Nazi slogans on walls and even organised demonstrations**.

• However, they were eventually caught, and their leaders were **guillotined in 1944**.

• Many young people refused to join the Hitler Youth movements and instead joined **rebel 'cultural' groups** that listened to banned 'degenerate' music and/or wore fashions which the Nazis condemned.

Q What did the White Rose Group do?

• Working-class groups such as **the Eidelweiss Pirates** or **the Meuten** taunted and even beat up members of the Hitler Youth.

Q Name two anti-Nazi youth groups.

• The more middle-class **Swing Movement** went to clubs with 'degenerate' music (for example, jazz and Swing) and dancing.

B Churches and the elites

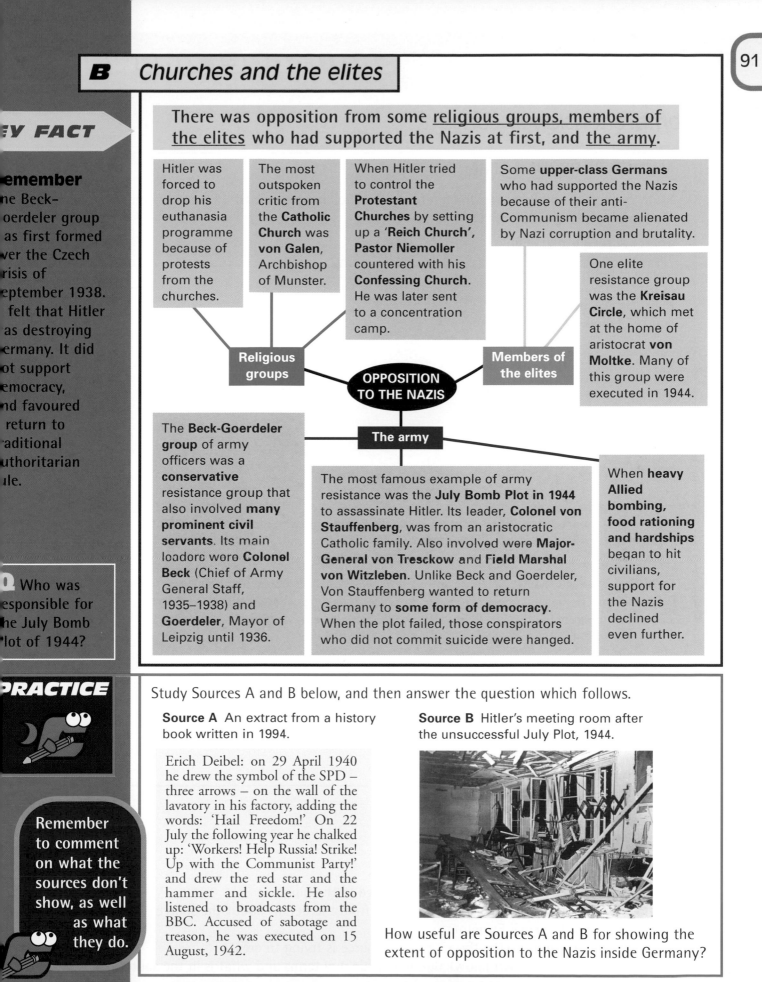

There was opposition from some <u>religious groups, members of the elites</u> who had supported the Nazis at first, and <u>the army</u>.

Hitler was forced to drop his euthanasia programme because of protests from the churches.

The most outspoken critic from the **Catholic Church** was **von Galen**, Archbishop of Munster.

When Hitler tried to control the **Protestant Churches** by setting up a '**Reich Church**', Pastor Niemoller countered with his **Confessing Church**. He was later sent to a concentration camp.

Some **upper-class Germans** who had supported the Nazis because of their anti-Communism became alienated by Nazi corruption and brutality.

One elite resistance group was the **Kreisau Circle**, which met at the home of aristocrat **von Moltke**. Many of this group were executed in 1944.

Religious groups

Members of the elites

OPPOSITION TO THE NAZIS

The army

The **Beck-Goerdeler group** of army officers was a **conservative** resistance group that also involved **many prominent civil servants**. Its main leaders were **Colonel Beck** (Chief of Army General Staff, 1935–1938) and **Goerdeler**, Mayor of Leipzig until 1936.

The most famous example of army resistance was the **July Bomb Plot in 1944** to assassinate Hitler. Its leader, **Colonel von Stauffenberg**, was from an aristocratic Catholic family. Also involved were **Major-General von Tresckow** and **Field Marshal von Witzleben**. Unlike Beck and Goerdeler, Von Stauffenberg wanted to return Germany to **some form of democracy**. When the plot failed, those conspirators who did not commit suicide were hanged.

When **heavy Allied bombing, food rationing and hardships** began to hit civilians, support for the Nazis declined even further.

KEY FACT

Remember
The Beck–Goerdeler group was first formed over the Czech crisis of September 1938. It felt that Hitler was destroying Germany. It did not support democracy, and favoured a return to traditional authoritarian rule.

Q Who was responsible for the July Bomb Plot of 1944?

PRACTICE

Remember to comment on what the sources don't show, as well as what they do.

Study Sources A and B below, and then answer the question which follows.

Source A An extract from a history book written in 1994.

Erich Deibel: on 29 April 1940 he drew the symbol of the SPD – three arrows – on the wall of the lavatory in his factory, adding the words: 'Hail Freedom!' On 22 July the following year he chalked up: 'Workers! Help Russia! Strike! Up with the Communist Party!' and drew the red star and the hammer and sickle. He also listened to broadcasts from the BBC. Accused of sabotage and treason, he was executed on 15 August, 1942.

Source B Hitler's meeting room after the unsuccessful July Plot, 1944.

How useful are Sources A and B for showing the extent of opposition to the Nazis inside Germany?

GERMANY, 1918–1945

Comprehension in context

MEDICINE THROUGH TIME

Study Sources A and B below, which refer to the cholera epidemic of 1831–1832, and then answer the question which follows.

Source A An illustration of 1832, showing the washing of a cholera victim's bedclothes in the Mill Stream, Exeter (this was also the city's main source of drinking water).

Source B An extract from the Report to the Leeds Board of Health, published in 1833, following a study of the cholera epidemic of 1831–1832.

> The Board will at once see how the disease (cholera) has been rampant in those parts of the town where there is often an entire lack of sewerage, drainage and paving. In one division of the town occupied entirely by cottage dwellings, including cellar dwellings, for 386 persons there are but two single privies. In such streets as these the Board will see the highest rate of cholera attacks.

Question

Explain, briefly, what you understand to be the significance of the terms:
a) 'drinking water' in Source A
b) 'privies' in Source B. *(4 marks)*

Answering this type of question

A What skills do I need?

You are expected to:

1 **give a clear definition** of any term(s) mentioned in the question
2 **extract information** from the source(s) and/or from the details about the source provided by the Principal Examiner
3 **comment on any impression** the writer of a source is trying to create
4 remember to **use your own knowledge** to explain any terms and what is in the source.

B Extra tips

In order to do well in exams you need to do more than just the minimum.

So follow these steps:

1 **Give some precise information** from the source itself (such as names) and/or from the attribution/ provenance details.
2 Remember to **add a few exact factual details from your own knowledge** to explain terms in the source(s), and what is being referred to/what perspective is shown etc. by **adding extra information.**

C Remember

- Make sure you read through your answer at some point to check that you have made specific references to the source(s) AND used your own knowledge.

- Such questions usually carry relatively low marks, so don't write half a page or more. Normally, two or three sentences, with a few precise, relevant comments and facts will be sufficient to obtain full marks.

Model answer

a) The reference to 'drinking water' is important because *the main method of spreading cholera was by contaminated drinking water – this was later shown by John Snow when he plotted the course of a cholera outbreak in Broad Street, London in 1854.* **Source A shows the bedclothes of a cholera victim being washed in the stream which was Exeter's main source of drinking water,** but this was in 1832, just after the disease had first hit Britain, and before Snow's discovery.

b) The reference to 'privies' is important as this was the main way drinking water was contaminated in the industrial towns and elsewhere. *The years 1831–1832 were the first time the disease had appeared in Britain. This led to Chadwick's Report in 1842 and, when cholera struck again in 1848,* *Parliament passed the first Public Health Act.* **Source B shows that there were only two privies (toilets) for 386 people in one of the worst areas of Leeds** – it was these overflowing cesspits that often contaminated the drinking water.

Why this answer scores full marks

- The parts in bold give **brief and accurate explanations of the importance of the two terms** – on their own, these would get the candidate half marks. In b), there is also a specific reference to the relevant source.

- The parts in italics add **extra information from the candidate's own knowledge** – these gain the extra two marks.

Recall questions

THE AMERICAN WEST, 1840–1895

Question

Describe the main steps in the development of the railroads during the 1860s.
(5 marks)

Answering this type of question

A What skills do I need?

You are expected to:

1 **give a clear explanation/show an overall grasp** of the aspect you have been asked to describe
2 use your own knowledge to **provide a detailed description with precise supporting facts**
3 try to **give a wider view/the overall context.**

B Remember

Look carefully at the marks available. Don't write a half a page or more if the question only carries two or three marks. If it carries five or six marks, write a couple of paragraphs.

Model answer

Before 1860, there had been some attempts to improve and speed up communications and travel between the east and west coasts of the USA. These included the use of steamboats, sea travel and stagecoaches – especially after 1848, when California became part of the USA following its defeat of Mexico.

By 1860, the US government had come to favour the building of a transcontinental railroad as the best way to unite the country. Initially, a southern route was surveyed, but this had to be abandoned when the American Civil War began in 1861. So instead, a central route was chosen – two companies (the Central Pacific and the Union Pacific Railroads) began to build from different points, to meet in the middle of the country. The government gave loans, grants and land to these two companies to help finance the building. The construction speeded up after the end of

the Civil War in 1865 and, in 1869, the two lines met at the Golden Spike Ceremony at Promontory Point in Utah. From 1870, other important rail routes were established (such as the Southern Pacific and the Northern Pacific), which helped development and expansion in the West.

Why this answer scores full marks

- The answer shows **clear understanding of the main developments** in the building of the railroads (the routes, the companies involved).

- There is **detailed supporting information** (dates, government help).

- There is a **developed explanation of their purpose** (to unite the USA after gaining new territory, and to speed up development of the West) and later developments.

Reliability/utility questions

GERMANY, 1918–1945

Source A An extract from a book written in 1940 by a former Nazi who left Germany in 1934. He is reporting a conversation he had in 1934 with a drunken Ernst Rohm, leader of the SA.

> Adolf is a swine. He is betraying all of us now. He is becoming friendly with army generals … We are revolutionaries, aren't we? The generals are a lot of old stick-in-the-muds. I am the centre of the new army, don't they see that?

Question

How useful is Source A as evidence about the threat the SA posed to Hitler in 1934? *(5 marks)*

Answering this type of question

A What skills do I need?

You are expected to:

1 comment on the **content/ information** given by the source(s)
2 use the **provenance/attribution information** provided, to **comment on the limitations** of the source(s).

B Remember

- If the question asks you to decide which of two (or more) sources is the most reliable/useful, you must **comment on ALL the sources AND make a choice**.

- If it is a utility question, make sure you mention the words **'useful'** or **'uses'** in your answer.

Model answer

Source A is useful to an extent because it shows that Rohm, the SA leader, was very angry in 1934. He wanted to be the head of a new German army, he hated the present generals and he believed that Hitler was betraying the Nazi Party. This was a threat as the SA had about two million members by 1934.

However, this source has reliability problems – it was written in 1940, six years after the conversation took place, and after the Night of the Long Knives. Maybe the writer didn't remember accurately what Rohm said, or he might be trying to justify Hitler's actions. Also, Rohm was drunk so might not have meant all he said. Hitler was very popular with many in the SA so not all of them would have supported Rohm.

Why this answer scores full marks

- It **deals with the content** (reasons why Rohm is angry).

- It **uses the provenance information** given in the caption (author, dates, the fact that Rohm was drunk).

- It is **balanced**, showing **limitations** as well as uses.

Cross-referencing questions

MEDICINE THROUGH TIME

Study Sources A, B and C below, which refer to the use of alternative medicine, and then answer the question which follows.

Source A An extract from a book about Chinese medicine, published in 1983, about an experiment carried out in 1959.

> In one experiment, 62 patients with stomach ulcers were observed and evaluated by doctors trained in Western methods, but treated by traditional Chinese methods.
>
> 53 (81.5%) recovered
>
> 7 (10.8%) showed some improvement
>
> 2 (3.1%) showed no change.

Source B An extract from a survey on the popularity of alternative medicine, based on 2000 participants.

Types of alternative therapy personally experienced	Tried by	Satisfied? Yes %	No %
Herbal medicine	12	73	18
Osteopathy	67	31	4
Massage	6	82	9
Homeopathy	4	66	16
Acupuncture	3	50	47
Chiropractic	2	68	19
Hypnotherapy	2	43	50
Psychotherapy	2	75	12

Source C An extract from a history textbook, published in 1995.

> Some doctors refer their patients to an alternative medical practitioner in cases where drugs have not had a permanent effect or where there is no need for surgery. Doctors often do this when they consider the problem not to be serious … Until very recently, doctors were extremely doubtful about its [acupuncture's] use. But during the past thirty years, doctors have become more familiar with it. Many have trained in its use … Many doctors remain doubtful about whether alternative medicine actually works. They point out that there is rarely any scientific proof to back the claims for cures.

Question

Does Source C support the evidence of Sources A and B about alternative medicine being as effective as modern 'high–tech' medicine? *(4 marks)*

Answering this type of question

A What skills do I need?

You are expected to:

1 **make clear/precise references** to ALL the sources mentioned – the references don't have to be long
2 try to **show how the sources are similar AND how they differ** (for example, extra facts, different figures).

B Remember

- Describing/copying out/rephrasing what the sources say/show **is NOT comparing them.**

- Once you've shown how they are similar, try to write a sentence beginning, 'However, although Source C says ... this is not supported by Source A, which...'

Model answer

Source C describes how some doctors refer patients to alternative medical practitioners. To an extent, this supports Source A as Source A shows that doctors trained in Western ('high-tech') methods have evaluated the effects of traditional Chinese methods. However, Source C doesn't say how successful alternative medicine is, unlike Source A, which shows that over 80 per cent of patients treated by the traditional methods recovered. In fact, Source C says that such alternative methods were often only used when drugs have not 'had a permanent effect' or where there is 'no need for surgery'. Source C also says that doctors often only use such methods when the problem is not seen as being 'serious', therefore implying that it isn't as effective as modern high-tech medicine. The source goes on to say how 'there is rarely any scientific proof to back the claims for cures' – this clearly contradicts Source A.

Source C also only supports Source B in a partial way, as Source B shows that in all types of alternative medicine except one (hypnotherapy) at least 50 per cent of those who have tried such methods were satisfied. This could suggest that such methods are successful but, as with Source A, Source C doesn't say anything positive about the successes or effectiveness of alternative medicine. In fact, it says 'many doctors remain doubtful' about whether it 'actually works'. However, to an extent, Source C does support Source B as Source C doubts the effectiveness of acupuncture, and Source B shows that only 50 per cent of patients using this method were satisfied.

Why this answer scores full marks

- There are **clear and supported** C–A and C–B cross-references (traditional/ alternative methods, degrees of success).

- As well as showing agreement, there is also an example of **how they differ.**

Source sufficiency questions

THE AMERICAN WEST, 1840–1895

Study Sources A and B below, which are about the reasons for Custer's defeat at the Battle of the Little Bighorn in 1876, and then answer the question which follows.

Source A An extract from a history textbook, published in 1998.

> Custer was determined to rout the Sioux with his own band of 265 men. His scouts had warned him that the Indian camp was huge, but Custer took no notice of their advice. In fact, 2500 warriors lay in wait for him. Custer was spotted on the hills high above the valley. He was soon surrounded by Sioux and Cheyenne warriors. Chief Gall of the Sioux, who had defeated Reno, attacked from the south. Crazy Horse and his warriors looped round from the north. The result was the biggest single defeat of the US army in the history of the West. Not one of Custer's soldiers survived. They were defeated by superior numbers of warriors who were better armed with the latest repeating rifles, and the foolishness of Custer's tactics.

Source B An impression by Kicking Bear, a Sioux warrior in the battle.

Question

Do Sources A and B provide enough information to explain why General Custer was defeated at the Battle of the Little Bighorn? Use the sources, and your own knowledge, to explain your answer. *(6 marks)*

Answering this type of question

A What skills do I need?

You are expected to:

1 **make use of all the sources** given, commenting on content AND any reliability problems
2 **give precise information/'other factors' from your own knowledge**, not contained in the sources.

B Remember

Use the sources AND your own knowledge. If you only do one of these things, you will only get half marks at most.

Model answer

Together, these sources only provide some of the reasons why Custer lost the Battle of the Little Bighorn. Source A is more helpful as it refers to the numbers involved, and shows how Custer's force of 265 was outnumbered by the 2500 Sioux and Cheyenne warriors. Source A also points out that the Indians were better armed than usual, with the latest repeating rifles, and it refers to the 'foolishness of Custer's tactics'. Source B is less useful in explaining why Custer was defeated as although it shows Custer's men surrounded, it doesn't show how greatly they were outnumbered. However, it does show the warriors using rifles, which confirms what Source A says.

Although both these sources give reasons why Custer was defeated, they do not give the full reasons. In particular, although Source A refers to Custer's 'foolish tactics', it doesn't explain what these were. In fact, the US army, which was fighting the Sioux in the War for the Black Hills, was commanded by General Sheridan and was several thousand strong. They knew that there were about 7000 Indians following Sitting Bull and Crazy Horse. Their plan was to attack the Indians from three directions, with sections led by Generals Crook, Gibbon and Terry. However, unknown to the other two, Crook's section was forced to retreat. But even then, Custer refused to wait until Gibbon and Terry were ready to attack, as he wanted to defeat the Sioux on his own with his 600 men. He split his own men into three groups, and ignored information from his scouts that the Indian camp in the valley of the Little Bighorn was huge.

Why this answer scores full marks

- **BOTH** the sources are used, and shown to give some reasons/explanations.

- The candidate's **own knowledge** is then used to provide more details and 'other factors'.

Analysis/explanation questions

GERMANY, 1918–1945

Question

Why did the Nazi Party place such importance on young people in Germany?
(6 marks)

Answering this type of question

A What skills do I need?

You are expected to:

1 give a **range of different reasons/explanations**
2 use **detailed own knowledge** to support each of the explanations given.

B Remember

- With 'why' (or 'how') questions, you need to explain **why** something happened not just describe what happened.

- Don't be satisfied with just one reason – try to give several different reasons.

- You must do more than just give a list of different reasons – so give detailed/precise supporting facts.

There were several reasons why the Nazis placed great importance on young people in Germany. One reason was because they wanted to control young people to ensure they would fulfil their 'proper' adult roles in the Third Reich and the war Hitler was planning. This was why the Hitler Youth organisations, run by von Schirach (who became Youth Leader of the Reich in 1933), stressed the importance of physical fitness for girls and boys – so women would be able to have many healthy babies (and so allow a large army) and boys would be fit soldiers and already have some military skills (such as map reading, marching and shooting).

Therefore, the Hitler Youth had different organisations for boys and girls, covering those aged 10 to 18. Sport, and military skills and attitudes, were emphasised on the many camps and outdoor events that members of the Hitler Youth had to attend. Those who got the best marks went to special schools such as the Adolf Hitler Schools and the Order Castles. Membership of the Hitler Youth was made compulsory in 1939. PE in schools was also given much more time under a new national curriculum drawn up and imposed by the Nazi Minister for Science and Education, Bernhard Rust.

The Nazis also wanted to control young people so that they would support their policies, especially that women should not have jobs (allowing unemployment of men to be reduced) and laws and actions against Jewish people. So lessons in biology not only stressed the 'natural role' of women, but also emphasised 'race science', which was designed to show Aryan superiority and Jewish inferiority. Support for this was not strong amongst German adults at first – the boycott of Jewish shops organised by the Nazis in 1933 was called off partly because many adults refused to follow it. In fact, the Nazis encouraged young people to report on adults (including teachers and even their parents) who said things against the Nazis – this stopped open opposition from adults, and allowed the Gestapo to identify many opponents.

However, there was also a more long-term reason why the Nazis wanted to control and influence young people – to ensure support for the Nazis into the future (the Third Reich was supposed to last 1000 years according to Hitler). Young people were easier to influence than adults (many of whom were socialists, Communists or liberals). If they could be successfully indoctrinated with Nazi ideas, then there would be very little opposition. So history in schools was rewritten to show how the Nazis were the saviours of Germany, and to show that democracy and socialism were bad. To make sure that young people did not come across ideas different from those pushed by the Nazis, all 'unreliable' teachers were sacked, and all those who remained had to swear loyalty to Hitler and join the Nazis' Teachers' League. However, despite all these efforts, not all young people supported the Nazis – many did not join the Hitler Youth, and others actively opposed them (such as the White Rose Group and the Eidelweiss Pirates).

Why this answer scores full marks

- **Several different explanations** are given, which are even separated into short- and long-term reasons.

- The answer is **well organised** – a rough plan has probably been worked out.

- There is also plenty of **precise supporting information** (dates, events).

Judgement/interpretation questions

MEDICINE THROUGH TIME

Study Sources A, B and C below, which are about the role played by the Christian religion in Britain during the Middle Ages, and then answer the question which follows.

Source A An extract from a history book by V. Coleman on the history of medicine, published in 1985.

> The close relationship between medicine and religion which had been thrown aside by Hippocrates was now back with a vengeance … The Christian religion, which dominated medical thinking, halted progress in Europe for the best part of a millennium.

Source B An extract from a history textbook published in 1996.

> The universities were controlled by the Church. They taught that the truth was mainly to be found by understanding books like the Bible or other writings from the past, like the books of Galen. The task of scholars was to make old ideas clear and not to start new ones.

Source C The title page of the 1493 edition of Mondino de Luzzi's *Anatomy*, written in 1316. It shows Mondino reading from a book while an assistant dissects a body.

Question

'The Christian religion dominated medical thinking and prevented any progress in medical knowledge in Europe throughout the Middle Ages.' Do you agree with this statement? Use the sources, and your own knowledge, to explain your answer.
(10 marks)

Answering this type of question

A What skills do I need?

You are expected to:

1 **use most of the sources** mentioned (if there are five or six, it isn't necessary to use all of them)
2 **add plenty of precise own knowledge** to add to what the sources give, and to mention aspects they don't
3 **produce a balanced answer** which looks at both sides AND provides a **range of issues/factors.**

B Remember

- You will only get half marks if you deal only with sources or own knowledge – you must do BOTH to score high marks.

- Make sure your facts are detailed – don't give general/vague references.

Model answer

I think this statement is only partly correct. Source A shows how there was a return to seeing the supernatural (in the case of the Christian religion, this was the belief in God sending illnesses as a punishment) as an explanation for the causes of illness. This was very similar to the ideas of the Ancient Egyptians and even prehistoric people, and marked a regression from the Ancient Greeks, such as Hippocrates and Aristotle, who stressed rational and more natural explanations and cures.

However, this regression was not just the result of Christianity. In fact, after the fall of Rome, much of the work of Hippocrates and Galen had been destroyed or lost in Europe – although it was preserved in the East, especially by the Islamic civilisation. But, when the Church began to reassert itself in Western Europe, it is true that illnesses and cures were mainly put down to God and the saints – there was great emphasis on prayers, the worship of saints and pilgrimages to holy shrines as ways of getting cures.

However, there were other aspects to the role of the Christian Church in medieval medicine. Source B shows, that as well as emphasising the Bible as a source of knowledge, the Church was also supporting the works of Galen (much of which were based on the earlier work of Hippocrates). It started to do this during the period 1000–1100. So it could be said that the Church helped medical knowledge recover from the setback brought about by the fall of Rome. The problem, though, was that until about 1200, the Church which, as Source B shows, controlled the universities, taught that the works of Galen were the absolute truth and so refused at first to accept any changes. This was important as Galen's work on human anatomy was mainly based on dissecting animals, and only some of his texts were recovered at first. But at first, the Church refused to allow human dissection.

However, as Source C shows, the attitude of the Church changed. From about 1300, it began to allow some dissection in universities, and even some revisions of Galen. This eventually led to important discoveries by Vesalius and Harvey. Before 1300, the Church had also encouraged the establishment of medical schools – the first one was in Salerno in Italy. Finally, the monasteries kept alive some aspects of Roman public health measures (clean drinking water and toilets) and set up hospitals for the care of the sick. So, overall, I disagree with the statement because although things were held back by the Church, some steps towards progress were also made.

• Go through these questions after you've revised a group of topics, putting a tick if you know the answer, a cross if you don't.

• Try these questions again the next time you revise … until you've got a column that's all ticks. Then you'll know you can be confident.

Part A: Medicine through time
Section 1: Medicine, 3000BC–AD500

1	What role did shamans play in prehistoric medicine?	☐ ☐ ☐
2	What was the connection between the trephining (trepanning) of skulls and prehistoric belief in the supernatural?	☐ ☐ ☐
3	What evidence suggests that patients survived the practice of trephining?	☐ ☐ ☐
4	Which god did Ancient Egyptians think gave doctors the power to heal?	☐ ☐ ☐
5	What important invention allowed Ancient Egyptians to record symptoms and treatments?	☐ ☐ ☐
6	How did Ancient Egyptian supernatural beliefs help lead to improved knowledge of human anatomy?	☐ ☐ ☐
7	Which god did Ancient Greeks believe to be the god of healing?	☐ ☐ ☐
8	Name one of this god's daughters.	☐ ☐ ☐
9	Which Ancient Greek doctor stressed the importance of clinical observation?	☐ ☐ ☐
10	Why was the city of Alexandria important in the development of medical knowledge in Ancient Greece?	☐ ☐ ☐
11	Name one public health measure taken by the Romans.	☐ ☐ ☐
12	Which Greek doctor in Ancient Rome built on the ideas of Hippocrates and Aristotle to develop the method of treatment by opposites?	☐ ☐ ☐
13	Why did this doctor make mistakes about human anatomy?	☐ ☐ ☐

Answers

1 Medicine men 2 Holes were drilled in skulls to allow evil spirits to escape 3 The bones healed over/continued growing after the operation 4 Thoth 5 Writing (hieroglyphics) 6 Mummification (extraction of organs) 7 Asclepios 8 Hygeia or Panacea 9 Hippocrates 10 It had a huge library/human dissection was allowed 11 One from: aqueducts/public toilets/public baths/draining of marshes (swamps) 12 Galen 13 Human dissection was banned (for religious reasons)/he used animals

Section 2: Medicine, 500–1750

14	Why did the fall of Rome lead to a regression in medicine in Europe?	☐ ☐ ☐
15	Which important Islamic doctor travelled from Baghdad to Greece to collect the medical texts of Hippocrates and Galen?	☐ ☐ ☐
16	How did Islamic governments help medicine progress?	☐ ☐ ☐
17	How did the medical ideas of the Islamic civilisation start to reach Europe?	☐ ☐ ☐
18	Name the Islamic doctor whose *Canon of Medicine* became the main medical textbook in Europe until 1700.	☐ ☐ ☐
19	How did the attitude of the Christian Church in the Middle Ages to the works of Hippocrates and Galen discourage progress?	☐ ☐ ☐
20	What did the Christian Church start to allow after about 1300?	☐ ☐ ☐
21	Which religious institutions made an important contribution to maintaining aspects of Roman public health?	☐ ☐ ☐
22	What illness hit Britain in 1348?	☐ ☐ ☐
23	What important invention during the Renaissance allowed the rapid spread of new and more accurate medical knowledge?	☐ ☐ ☐
24	How did the Reformation during the sixteenth century help further advances in medical knowledge?	☐ ☐ ☐
25	Who, in 1531, was able to bring out a much more accurate book on human anatomy (*On Anatomical Procedures*), based on new and more complete translations, from Arabic into Latin, of the works of Galen?	☐ ☐ ☐
26	Name the man who, in the 1530s and 1540s, found several errors in the works of Galen on anatomy.	☐ ☐ ☐
27	Who, in his book *On the Motion of the Heart and Blood* in 1628, proved Galen's theories on circulation were wrong?	☐ ☐ ☐
28	What important invention in 1693, during the Scientific Revolution, later led to important breakthroughs in medicine?	☐ ☐ ☐

Answers

14 Books and libraries (including medical books) were destroyed/there was a return to a more primitive outlook 15 Hunain ibn Ishaq (Johannitus) 16 They set up medical schools/insisted that doctors have licences/took public health measure/set up hospitals 17 By trade and the Crusades 18 Ibn Sina (Avicenna) 19 It said their work was the absolute truth (although in fact only some of their books had been recovered by then) 20 Human dissection in universities 21 Monasteries 22 The Black Death (bubonic plague) 23 Printing 24 It weakened the power/control of the Church and religion, including over education 25 Johannes Guinter 26 Vesalius 27 William Harvey 28 The microscope

Section 3: Medicine, 1750 to present

29 What area of medicine suffered a set-back as a result of the early impact of the Industrial Revolution?	□	□	□
30 What positive impact did the Industrial Revolution have later?	□	□	□
31 Who published his discoveries concerning vaccination against smallpox in 1798?	□	□	□
32 What important discovery was made by Louis Pasteur in 1857?	□	□	□
33 How did the Franco-Prussian War, 1870–1871, help speed up developments in medicine?	□	□	□
34 What was the name of Pasteur's great German rival?	□	□	□
35 Name the German scientist who was the first to use anti-toxins to fight a human disease (diphtheria) in 1891.	□	□	□
36 What was the name of the scientist who began the search for a chemical 'magic bullet' to fight disease in humans?	□	□	□
37 For what disease did this person find such a cure in 1909–1911?	□	□	□
38 Who discovered a second 'magic bullet' to fight blood poisoning, in 1932?	□	□	□
39 What type of chemical was the main active ingredient of this 'magic bullet'?	□	□	□
40 What human disease did M&B 693 combat?	□	□	□
41 What important discovery was made by Alexander Fleming in 1928?	□	□	□
42 What important development was made by Howard Florey and Ernst Chain?	□	□	□
43 What event in December 1941 finally got Florey and Chain the funds and equipment they needed for the mass production of this drug?	□	□	□
44 When did the Labour government establish the National Health Service to provide health care for all?	□	□	□
45 What problem has now arisen with antibiotics such as penicillin?	□	□	□

Answers

29 Public health 30 Better equipment and chemicals
31 Edward Jenner 32 That germs caused infection/disease
33 The nationalism led to rivalry, with governments funding institutions and research teams 34 Robert Koch 35 Emil von Behring 36 Paul Ehrlich 37 Syphilis 38 Gerhard Domagk
39 Sulphonamide 40 Pneumonia 41 Penicillium mould/ penicillin killed bacteria without harming human tissue or having side-effects 42 How to make pure penicillin 'mould juice' 43 Pearl Harbor – this led the US government to give the necessary funds 44 1948 45 Bacteria becoming resistant (the 'super bugs')

Section 4: Themes in medicine

46	What impact did the growing professionalism of medical training in the Middle Ages have on the role of women?
47	What invention in about 1620 led to women being excluded from midwifery?
48	What medical roles did women continue to play despite being excluded from formal medicine?
49	Name the woman who brought a form of inoculation to Britain in 1718.
50	Whose activities during the Crimean War did much to improve nursing as a medical profession?
51	Name the first British woman to qualify, in 1870, as a doctor (at the University of Paris).
52	What important step for equality for women in medicine took place in Britain in 1876?
53	What act of 1919 helped to establish nursing as a high-status profession?
54	During the Middle Ages, what town organisation was usually responsible for public health issues?
55	What disease flared up in London during 1665–1666?
56	What new disease, which first hit Britain in 1831, finally led to the passing of the first Public Health Act in 1848?
57	What did the new Labour government introduce in 1948?
58	What were the three main problems of surgery?
59	Which sixteenth-century surgeon made some important advances?
60	What anaesthetics were discovered, respectively, in 1842 and 1847?
61	What was the 'Black Period of Surgery'?
62	Who, using Pasteur's germ theory, used carbolic acid as the first antiseptic?
63	What discovery by Karl Landsteiner in 1901 led to successful blood transfusions?

Answers

46 Their gradual exclusion from the formal practice of medicine 47 Obstetric (delivery) forceps 48 Housewife-physicians and 'wise women' 49 Lady Mary Wortley Montagu 50 Florence Nightingale 51 Elizabeth Garrett 52 All medical qualifications were opened to women 53 The Registration of Nurses Act 54 Corporations (made up of rich men) 55 Bubonic plague 56 Cholera 57 The NHS 58 Pain, infection, bleeding 59 Ambroise Paré 60 Ether, chloroform 61 The years 1846–1870, when longer operations (allowed by anaesthetics) led to increased death rates because of infection (there were still no antiseptics) 62 Joseph Lister 63 Different blood groups

Part B: The American West, 1840–1895
Section 1: Developments before 1840

1	Where did the first whites settle in America?	☐	☐	☐
2	When did the USA became independent?	☐	☐	☐
3	What huge area, stretching west from the Mississippi to the Rocky Mountains, and containing the Great Plains, did the USA purchase from France in 1803?	☐	☐	☐
4	Why were the Great Plains often known as the 'Great American Desert'?	☐	☐	☐
5	What was the 'Permanent Indian Frontier'?	☐	☐	☐
6	What name is given to the early nineteenth-century belief of many white Americans that they had the right to settle all land west of the Mississippi and to 'civilise' the Native Americans living in the 'Indian Territory' they had previously 'granted' to them?	☐	☐	☐
7	Name one of the five most important nations of the Plains Indians.	☐	☐	☐
8	What was 'counting coup'?	☐	☐	☐
9	What kind of warfare was practised by the Plains Indians?	☐	☐	☐
10	How was their attitude to land different from that held by most whites?	☐	☐	☐
11	Which animal was central to the Plains Indians' way of life?	☐	☐	☐
12	Who were the 'mountain men'?	☐	☐	☐
13	Why did many of these men become trailblazers after 1840?	☐	☐	☐
14	Name the two most important trails 'blazed' west by mountain men in the early 1840s.	☐	☐	☐
15	Why were many whites eager to move west across the Great Plains after 1840?	☐	☐	☐

Answers

1 Along the east coast 2 1783 3 Louisiana 4 Large parts in the south often had droughts in summer/much of it was in the rainshadows of the Appalachian Mountains in the East and the Rocky Mountains in the West 5 The line, west of the Mississippi, decided by the US government to mark the border between the USA and 'Indian Territory' (in 1834, it was fixed along the 95th meridian) 6 Manifest Destiny 7 One from: Sioux/Cheyenne/Crow/Comanche/Apache 8 Running/ galloping up to an enemy warrior and touching him with a 'coup stick', to gain honour 9 Short, fierce, but limited, low-intensity/'sustainable' warfare 10 They believed it belonged to the people as a whole so couldn't be owned by individuals or families (and should be passed on in a good state to future generations) 11 Buffalo/bison 12 The early fur traders, trappers and hunters 13 The fur trade was declining. 14 Santa Fe, Oregon 15 The 1837 financial crisis in the East/ the land shortage and high prices

Section 2: Developments 1840–1895

16 Which three areas did the USA gain, respectively, in 1845, 1846 and 1848?	☐ ☐ ☐
17 What discovery in California in 1848 led to a great increase in the numbers of people wanting to go west?	☐ ☐ ☐
18 What improvement in communications between East and West in 1869 led to increased development of the West by helping farmers, cattle ranchers and the growth of towns?	☐ ☐ ☐
19 How did this affect the life of the Plains Indians?	☐ ☐ ☐
20 What, in the early cattle industry, was the 'Long Drive'?	☐ ☐ ☐
21 When did the US government pass the Homestead Act in order to encourage more people to settle and farm on the Great Plains?	☐ ☐ ☐
22 What problem did homesteaders face from cattle ranching?	☐ ☐ ☐
23 What invention of 1874 helped solve this problem, and also ended the 'open range'?	☐ ☐ ☐
24 Why were miners' courts and vigilance committees often set up in the early years of the West?	☐ ☐ ☐
25 What important 'range war' lasted from 1877 to 1881?	☐ ☐ ☐
26 What treaty of 1851, between the US government and the chiefs of the main tribes of the Great Plains, established large reservations for each tribe, in return for them leaving open the important routes west (thus ending the policy of 'one big reservation')?	☐ ☐ ☐
27 Identify one of the problems experienced by Indians on these reservations.	☐ ☐ ☐
28 What was the Great Plains Massacre of the 1870s?	☐ ☐ ☐
29 Why did the war for the Black Hills take place in the years 1875–1877?	☐ ☐ ☐
30 What battle was won by the Sioux and Cheyenne in 1876?	☐ ☐ ☐
31 What event in 1890 effectively ended the Plains Wars?	☐ ☐ ☐

Answers

16 Texas, Oregon, California 17 Gold (leading to the California Gold Rush) 18 The completion of the first East–West railroad 19 This (and later railroads) disrupted the great buffalo herds and led to more settlers 20 This was when cattle were rounded up in Texas and moved north to the cow towns 21 1862 22 Cattle wandered across/destroyed their crops 23 Barbed wire (allowing cheaper/easier fencing) 24 Lack of sufficient law officers/slow decisions because of the distance from Washington 25 The Lincoln County War 26 Fort Laramie 27 One from: poor land for crops/poor hunting/inadequate food/pressure to abandon language and religious beliefs/allowances not paid/corrupt or inefficient agents 28 The US government's deliberate attempt to force Indians to stop hunting by the wholesale slaughter of the buffalo 29 Gold was discovered in the Black Hills, which the Sioux refused to sell, but white settlers/miners still came 30 Little Bighorn 31 The Massacre at Wounded Knee

Part C: Germany, 1918–1945
Section 1: 1918–1933

1	What impact did the Allied naval blockade have on Germany?	☐ ☐ ☐
2	At which German naval base, in October 1918, did a mutiny spark off uprisings which quickly spread to other ports and towns?	☐ ☐ ☐
3	What was the name of the revolutionary socialist group which launched an unsuccessful workers' revolution in Berlin in December 1918?	☐ ☐ ☐
4	What were the Freikorps?	☐ ☐ ☐
5	What did Article 48 of the new Weimar Constitution allow?	☐ ☐ ☐
6	Why did many Germans see the Weimar politicians as the 'November Criminals'?	☐ ☐ ☐
7	Why did French and Belgian troops occupy the Ruhr in 1923?	☐ ☐ ☐
8	Who were the SA?	☐ ☐ ☐
9	Why was Hitler imprisoned in 1924?	☐ ☐ ☐
10	Name the German politician who led Germany into what was called the 'Golden Years'.	☐ ☐ ☐
11	What did the Dawes Plan of 1924 and the Young Plan of 1929 do?	☐ ☐ ☐
12	Why did Hitler feel it necessary to reorganise the Nazi Party in 1925, when he came out of prison?	☐ ☐ ☐
13	Who headed Nazi Party propaganda?	☐ ☐ ☐
14	What event in October 1929 ended US loans to Germany, and resulted in the Depression and over six million German unemployed by 1932?	☐ ☐ ☐
15	When did the Nazis become the largest single party in the German Reichstag (parliament)?	☐ ☐ ☐
16	Which German politician persuaded Hindenburg to appoint Hitler as Chancellor in January 1933?	☐ ☐ ☐

Answers

1 Serious food shortages/hunger and unrest 2 Kiel
3 The Spartacist League/Spartacists 4 A paramilitary force of right-wing, unemployed ex-soldiers 5 Allowed the President to bypass the Reichstag and rule by decree in an emergency 6 Because they had signed the armistice in November 1918, and then signed the Treaty of Versailles (the Kaiser and army High Command had kept defeats secret and had instead led Germans to think they were winning the war) 7 The German government had said it couldn't pay the second reparations instalment 8 The Stormtroopers (Brownshirts), set up in 1921, were Nazi thugs who beat up left-wing opponents and attacked their meetings, demonstrations, etc. Ernst Rohm soon became their leader 9 In November 1923, when the German government had called off its passive resistance to the French occupation of the Ruhr, Hitler had tried, unsuccessfully, to overthrow the government (the Beer Hall/Munich Putsch) 10 Gustav Stresemann 11 Gave US loans to help German industry/reduced the total figure and extended the time-scale of reparations payments 12 While Hitler had been in prison following his failed Beer Hall Putsch, the party had been banned, and had split into opposing factions/there was little support for extremist parties during the 'Golden Years' 13 Josef Goebbels 14 The Wall Street Crash 15 July 1932 16 von Papen

Section 2: 1933–1945

17	What event took place in February 1933, just before new elections were due in March?
18	What act did Hitler and the Nazis push through the Reichstag in March 1933?
19	Why did Hitler order the Night of the Long Knives in which Rohm and other SA leaders were murdered by the SS in June 1934?
20	Which two organisations were controlled by Heinrich Himmler?
21	Who drew up a 'New Plan' that was part of Nazi attempts to reduce unemployment?
22	Why did this person resign from the government in 1937?
23	What Nazi organisation replaced the free trade unions which the Nazis had abolished in May 1933?
24	Name one of the two schemes it ran.
25	What were the '3 Ks'?
26	What was the Motherhood Cross System designed to do?
27	Name one of the three subjects emphasised in the new national curriculum for schools drawn up and imposed by the Nazis.
28	Who became the Youth Leader of the Reich in July 1933?
29	When did membership of the Hitler Youth become compulsory?
30	What were the Nuremberg Laws of 1935?
31	What was decided at the Wannsee Conference in January 1942?
32	Name one group of German youths who resisted the Nazi dictatorship.
33	How was the Beck-Goerdeler group different from von Stauffenberg's group?

Answers

17 Reichstag Fire – blamed on the Communists
18 The Enabling Act (this made it much easier to destroy Weimar democracy) 19 Rohm and the more militant sections of the Nazi Party were pushing for the fulfilment of the 'left' policies in the party programme/the regular army were angry at Rohm's demands for the SA to be the new army
20 The SS and the Gestapo 21 Schacht 22 He felt the drive for rearmament, and Goring's Four-Year Plan, were undermining his work and leading to economic collapse
23 The German Labour Front (DAF) 24 The Beauty of Labour or Strength Through Joy 25 Kinder, Kirche, Kuche, i.e. the traditional roles for women 26 To encourage women to have large families (by awarding gold, silver or bronze medals according to the number of children) 27 One of: history/biology/PE 28 von Schirach 29 1939 30 A set of anti-Jewish laws, which included the removal of German citizenship from Jews and the prohibition of inter-marriage 31 The 'Final Solution' (mass extermination or genocide) of all Jews in Europe (the Holocaust) 32 One from: the White Rose Group/the Edelweiss Pirates/the Meuten/the Swing Movement 33 The Beck-Goerdeler group wanted authoritarian rule (as under the Kaiser), while von Stauffenberg wanted a return to some form of democracy

- Fill in the gaps as you revise to test your understanding.
- You could photocopy these pages if you wanted to do this more than once.
- You'll also end up with a concise set of notes on some of the most important ideas.

Part A: *Medicine through time*

Prehistoric medicine

The evidence suggests that prehistoric people had a _____ approach to medicine, based on supernatural beliefs and common-sense treatments.

Trephining of skulls was probably a 'cure' for possession by _____ _____ .

Ancient Egyptian medicine

The Ancient Egyptians invented a method of writing known as _____ .

They believed that the god _____ gave doctors the skill to cure the ill.

The practice of 'mummification' led to increased knowledge of human _____ .

Medicine in Ancient Greece

In Ancient Greece, the god of healing was known as _____ .

_____ had a more rational approach to illness, and stressed the idea of clinical observation.

The Theory of the Four _____ was based on the belief that the human body was made up of four liquids.

Alexandria was important because, for a time, it allowed _____ of human bodies.

Roman medicine

The Romans made several important developments in _____ _____ , such as aqueducts, public toilets and sewers.

Building on the work of Hippocrates, _____ based his cures on the theories of balance and treatment by opposites.

Islamic medicine

After the fall of Rome, much of the medical knowledge of the ancient world was _____ in the new Islamic Arabic civilisation in the Middle East.

_____ _____ (aka Avicenna) wrote the *Canon of Medicine*, which later was translated into Latin and became the main medical textbook in Europe until 1700.

Medieval medicine

The works of Hippocrates and Galen returned to Europe as a result of the Crusades and increased _____ with the Islamic world.

The first medical school in medieval Europe was set up in _____ .

From about 1300, the Church began to allow some public _____ in universities.

One of the biggest problems during the Middle Ages was the public health of towns. In 1346–1350, the _____ _____ swept across Europe.

Renaissance medicine

The Renaissance, and then the Reformation, weakened Church control of _____ .

During the Renaissance, there was a more _____ approach, based on close observation and recording.

In 1531, Guinter brought out a translation of a newly discovered book by _____ on anatomy. This was a significant improvement on what had been available during the Middle Ages.

However, mistakes in Galen's anatomy were discovered by _____ ; at first, though, he did not publish his findings.

Some important developments in surgery were made by _____ , but most doctors stuck to the old methods.

As medicine became increasingly professional, the formal role of _____ in medicine was reduced.

The Industrial Revolution

One of the effects of the Scientific Revolution had been a greater _____ for physicians and doctors.

As a result of the Industrial Revolution, medicine eventually benefited from better equipment and chemicals. This allowed further discoveries and _____ .

In 1798, Jenner published the results of his work on smallpox. He called his method of combating the disease _____ .

The next great discovery was by _____ , who was able to show how germs caused disease.

In 1891, von Behring was the first to cure an ill human using an _____-_____.

The drugs revolution

Ehrlich was the first to develop a chemical '_____ _____' against the microbes causing disease (syphilis, 1909).

The next breakthrough was in 1932, when _____ used a sulphonamide to cure blood poisoning.

The first antibiotic – penicillin – was discovered in 1928 by _____ .

The problem of how to mass produce penicillin was not overcome until the _____ _____ _____ , when Florey and Chain were given sufficient funds and equipment.

Medicine now

In 1948, the _____ _____ _____ was set up, to provide free medical treatment for all.

One problem with 'high-tech' medicine has been the _____-_____ of certain drugs, such as Thalidomide and Largactil.

Because of the problems associated with modern medicine, there has been a big revival of interest in _____ medicine, such as herbal medicine and acupuncture.

Women and medicine

In the civilisations of the ancient world, women were allowed to train and practise as doctors, especially to treat other _____ .

During the Middle Ages in Europe, women became increasingly _____ from formal medicine.

The invention of the obstetric forceps led to women even being excluded from _____ .

Because trained doctors were few and expensive, most people continued to rely on informal medical practitioners, such as _____-_____ and local 'wise women'.

Women began to return to formal medicine after 1850 – at first, as a result of the improvements in _____ brought about by Florence Nightingale.

_____ _____ was the first British woman to qualify as a doctor (in 1870), although she had to go to Paris to do so.

In _____ , all medical qualifications in Britain were opened to women.

Public health

After the fall of Rome, practical measures for public health disappeared rapidly during what became known as the '_____ _____' .

In the Middle Ages, public health measures were left to the _____ of each town – these rich men did not see pubic health as their responsibility.

By-laws to force people to clear away rubbish and empty overflowing cesspits were usually only made when there was a serious outbreak of _____ .

It took the appearance of a new disease – _____ – in 1831, to begin a change in attitude of governments to public health actions.

As a result of _____'s report in 1842, a Public Health Act was passed in 1848.

In 1854, _____ discovered the link between contaminated water and cholera. This was later confirmed by the discoveries about _____ made by Pasteur and Koch.

Surgery

The three major problems associated with surgery were: _____ , _____ and _____ .

For a long time, surgery had a low _____ in medicine – and was often left to untrained _____-_____.

Year	Anaesthetic	Discoverer
1799		Humphrey Davy
	ether	Crawford Long
1847	chloroform	

The period 1846–1870 is often known as the '_____ _____' of surgery, because of the increased death rates after anaesthetics allowed longer and more complicated surgery.

In _____, Joseph Lister began to use _____ _____ as an antiseptic.

In 1887, Neuber and Bergmann in Germany invented _____ techniques by sterilising instruments and clothes.

In 1901, Landsteiner's discovery of _____ _____ led to successful blood transfusions.

The horrific injuries caused by modern weapons led to the development of _____ surgery by doctors such as Gillies and McIndoe.

Part B: The American West, 1840–1895

The USA and the West

The USA gained its independence from Britain in _____ .

In 1803, the USA bought _____ from France.

The Great Plains stretched from the Mississippi River in the East to the Rocky Mountains in the _____ .

In 1834, the US government declared all land west of the _____ meridian to be 'Indian Territory'.

The Plains Indians

The Lakota, Nakota and Dakota were the main sub-groups of the _____ nation of Native Americans.

Warriors of the Plains Indians often proved their bravery by 'counting _____' against an enemy.

The life of the Plains Indians centred on the _____ , although other animals were also hunted.

Shamans were holy men or _____ men believed to have special religious powers.

Pioneers and wagon trains

The early fur trappers, hunters and traders were often known as '_____ _____'.

When the fur trade began to collapse in the late 1830s, many of these men helped 'blaze' _____ to the West, across the Great Plains.

'_____ _____' was the belief held by many whites that the USA needed to spread across the Great Plains to the west coast, to form one big country.

Date	New territory gained by the USA
1845	
	Oregon
1848	

The Gold Rush and the railways

The discovery of gold in 1848 in _____ led thousands of miners to take part in a gold rush to the West.

In _____, at the Golden Spike Ceremony, the Central Pacific and Union Pacific Railroads met at Promontory Point, Utah.

Cattle and cowboys

The '_____ _____' was when cattle were taken north from Texas to the main rail towns.

The cattle trade boom was ended, in part, by two severe _____ in 1886 and 1887.

Homesteaders

The US government tried to encourage people to settle on the Great Plains by passing the _____ Act in 1862.

Problems often arose between homesteaders and cattle ranchers when cattle on the 'open range' destroyed crops – the invention of _____ _____ in 1874 helped homesteaders fence off their land.

Law and order

Apart from gunslingers and outlaw gangs, one problem was the conflict between homesteaders and cattle 'barons'. This sometimes led to 'range wars' such as:

Date	Range war
1877–81	
	Johnson County War

The struggle for the Great Plains

The Indian Removal Act, _____ , forced all tribes east of the Mississippi to move into the 'Indian Territory' west of the river because, at first, US government policy was based on the idea of one great 'Indian _____'.

Increasing conflicts with the Plains Indians led to the signing of the Treaty of Fort _____ in 1851, which ended the previous policy and instead split the Indian tribes up into separate individual reservations, which whites were not to enter.

The Plains Wars, 1860–1890

Conflict on the South and Central Plains, as more whites crossed or settled on the Great Plains, led to several new treaties:

Date	Treaty
1861	
	Medicine Lodge Creek
1869	

The _____ _____ Massacre was when, in the 1870s, the US government supported the wholesale slaughter of the buffalo to force the Plains Indians to accept new terms.

The War for the North Plains was triggered by the discovery of _____ in the remote North-West and by the subsequent building of the Bozeman Trail in 1866 (in breach of the 1851 Treaty).

Custer was defeated at the Battle of the _____ _____ in 1876.

The Plains Wars were effectively ended by the Massacre at _____ _____ in December 1890.

Part C: Germany 1918–1945

Changes in Germany

By 1918, the Allied _____ _____ was causing serious food shortages in Germany.

In December 1918, the Spartacist League tried to start a revolution in Berlin, but this was crushed by the army and the _____ .

Weimar Germany, 1919–1923

In 1918, many Germans had liked the authoritarian rule of the Kaiser and disliked _____, which they saw as a foreign idea imposed by the Allies.

In 1923, France and Belgium invaded the Ruhr because Germany said it was unable to pay its second _____ instalment. This led to the collapse of the German currency and _____-_____ .

The founding of the Nazi Party

In 1921, _____ had become leader of the Nazi Party.

Once he was leader, Hitler set up the _____ (SA) to attack left-wing meetings and demonstrations.

In November _____ , Hitler's attempted 'Beer Hall Putsch' in Munich failed, and he was imprisoned.

Germany before the Depression

Under the leadership of Gustav _____ , Germany soon recovered from the problems arising from the occupation of the Ruhr and experienced what became known as the _____ _____ .

During this period, support for extreme parties _____ , and the Nazis experienced their 'Lean Years'.

Much of Germany's recovery in the 1920s, however, was based on loans from the _____ .

The Nazis come to power

The US loans to Germany stopped after the _____ _____ _____ . By 1932, unemployment had risen to ____ million.

Because coalition governments found it difficult to agree on what action to take, President Hindenburg increasingly ruled by _____ , as allowed by Article 48 of the _____ Constitution.

Growing violence by Nazi Stormtroopers, led by Ernst _____ , and Hitler's assurances to wealthy _____ , led to Hitler's appointment as Chancellor in January _____ .

The Nazi dictatorship

The Reichstag Fire helped Hitler push the _____ ____ through the Reichstag in March 1933. By July, it had been used to establish a Nazi dictatorship.

Nazi power was maintained by the terror carried out by the Gestapo and the SS, which were both under the control of Heinrich _____ .

The Nazis also maintained control through the skilful use of censorship and propaganda, directed by Josef _____ , who was Minister of Propaganda and Culture.

Nazi economic policy

Nazi economic policies reduced _____ . This also helped the Nazis maintain support.

The Nazi government funded a programme of _____ _____ , rearmament and conscription to reduce unemployment.

At first, economic policy was run by _____ , who drew up a 'New Plan'.

The Nazi 'Volksgemeinschaft'

Nazi policy for women was based on the '____ _____': Kinder, Kirche, Kuche (Children, Church, Kitchen).

In _____ , membership of the Hitler Youth was made compulsory.

Outside the Nazi 'community'

Once the Nazis had gained control of Germany, they immediately began to take measures against _____ people, who they believed were inferior to the 'Aryan' race.

Year	Action/policy
1933	Boycott of Jewish shops
	Jews sacked from the civil service, law, the media and education
	Jews banned from all public facilities
	Nuremberg Laws (taking away citizenship, forbidding inter-marriage)
1938	_____ _____ (attacks on Jewish homes, shops and synagogues)

At the Wannsee Conference, 1942, leading Nazis decided on the '_____ _____' .

Opposition

Many Germans remained opposed to the Nazis – the _____ _____ _____ (a group of students at Munich University) distributed anti-Nazi leaflets and organised demonstrations, until their leaders were executed in 1944.

The Rote Kapelle (Red Orchestra) was a group of German _____ who passed military secrets to the USSR during the Second World War.

The July Bomb Plot in 1944 was led by von _____ .

Part A: Medicine through time

Prehistoric medicine
dual/evil spirits

Ancient Egyptian medicine
hieroglyphics/Thoth/anatomy

Medicine in Ancient Greece
Asclepios/Hippocrates/Humours/dissection

Roman medicine
public health/Galen

Islamic medicine
preserved/Ibn Sina

Medieval medicine
trade/Salerno/dissection/Black Death (bubonic plague)

Renaissance medicine
education/scientific/Galen/Vesalius/Paré/women

The Industrial Revolution
status (respect)/progress/vaccination/Pasteur/anti-toxin

The drugs revolution
magic bullet/Domagk/Fleming/Second World War

Medicine now
National Health Service (NHS)/side-effects/alternative

Women and medicine
women/excluded/midwifery/housewife-physicians/nursing/Elizabeth Garrett/1876

Public health
Dark Ages/corporation/disease/cholera/Chadwick/Snow/germs

Surgery
pain/infection/bleeding/status/barber-surgeons/laughing gas (nitrous oxide)/1842/James Simpson/Black Period/1867/carbolic acid/aseptic/blood groups/plastic

Part B: The American West, 1840–1895

The USA and the West
1783/Louisiana/West/95th

The Plains Indians
Sioux/coup/buffalo/medicine

Pioneers and wagon trains
mountain men/trails/Manifest Destiny/Texas/1846/California

The Gold Rush and the railways
California/1869

Cattle and cowboys
Long Drive/winters

Homesteaders
Homestead/barbed wire

Law and order
Lincoln County War/1892

The struggle for the Great Plains
1830/reservation/Laramie

The Plains Wars, 1860–1890
Fort Lyon (Fort Wise)/1867/Fort Cobb/Great Plains/gold/Little Bighorn/Wounded Knee

Part C: Germany, 1918–1945

Changes in Germany
naval blockade/Freikorps

Weimar Germany, 1919–1923
democracy/reparations/hyper-inflation

The founding of the Nazi Party
Hitler/Stormtroopers/1923

Germany before the Depression
Stresemann/Golden Years/declined/USA

The Nazis come to power
Wall Street Crash/six/decree/Weimar/Rohm/industrialists (businessmen)/1933

The Nazi dictatorship
Enabling Act/Himmler/Goebbels

Nazi economic policy
unemployment/public works/Schacht

The Nazi 'Volksgemeinschaft'
3 Ks/1939

Outside the Nazi 'community'
Jewish/1933/1934/1935/Crystal Night (Kristallnacht or Night of Broken Glass)/Final Solution

Opposition
White Rose Group/Communists/Stauffenberg

Medicine through time

Prehistoric medicine

1   Source A shows a large, smooth, round hole in the skull – it's not jagged, therefore it is not likely to be the result of an accident. Because the bone has grown after the hole was cut, it shows that prehistoric people could perform surgery successfully but, with no written evidence, we cannot tell why it was done.

Source B only shows a medicine man – it doesn't show any cures. But, Native Americans lived a similar life to prehistoric nomadic hunters and used various methods to drive away 'evil spirits'. So maybe prehistoric medicine was based on similar beliefs (although we cannot be certain).

Ancient Egyptian medicine

Their religious beliefs helped medical progress as mummification gave knowledge of human anatomy, while cleanliness and hygiene were also stressed. Religion hindered progress as doctors who departed from cures passed down by the gods were punished, and studying the organs removed during mummification was banned.

Medicine in Ancient Greece

The source shows the god of healing – it tells us that, in 350BC, the Ancient Greeks believed in supernatural causes and cures for illnesses. It does not say anything about the more practical, natural forms of healing which were used in the Asclepions built as part of the cult of Asclepios.

From Hippocrates to Aristotle

1   Aristotle.
2   Dissection of human bodies was allowed (this increased knowledge of anatomy), and a huge library of medical books was set up. Also, doctors were trained in surgery and medicine; and close, clinical observation was stressed. Doctors trained there then spread such ideas all over the Mediterranean world.

Roman medicine (1)

1   Julius Caesar.
2   Any two from: aqueducts for clean drinking water/public baths/public toilets/sewers/draining of swamps.

Roman medicine (2)

Source A tells us that dissection of humans and close observation took place in Ancient Greece at Alexandria, and that this led to advances in knowledge of human anatomy. However, in Source B, we see Galen dissecting a pig – he believed that by dissecting some animals (pigs, dogs, barbary apes), he could gain extra knowledge about human anatomy. He did this because human dissection was banned for religious reasons in Ancient Rome. Although he had trained at Alexandria, by then dissection was no longer allowed. This led to him making several mistakes. Because he wrote many books that survived the fall of Rome, doctors followed his ideas for the next 1400 years.

Islamic medicine

The source shows a Caesarean operation being performed on a pregnant woman, and indicates that this operation was known to doctors in the civilisations of the ancient world. This shows continuity, and suggests that Islamic doctors could perform such operations. However, it doesn't tell us how successful they were, and it only shows male doctors, although female doctors did exist and usually dealt with female patients.

Medieval medicine

1   The Church gradually accepted the works of Hippocrates and Galen (which had been lost in Europe since the fall of Rome) and had them translated from Arabic into Latin. It later helped establish medical schools (for example, Salerno) and even allowed some dissection from about 1300.
2   It also stressed supernatural causes and cures of illness, and insisted that the ideas of Hippocrates and Galen were the total truth and so banned changes; dissection was also banned for a long time.

Public heath in the Middle Ages

1   Monasteries and hospitals.
2   It was bubonic plague, spread by the fleas of black rats.

Renaissance medicine (1)

1   There was a strong insistence on going back to original texts from Ancient Greece and Rome, so avoiding later mistakes and misunderstandings in translations. But there was also a new and more scientific approach based on close observation (for example, more accurate human anatomy by Vesalius), and the invention of printing helped spread knowledge. The religious Reformation also weakened Church control of education, including medical training.
2   Vesalius.

Renaissance medicine (2)

1   William Harvey's.
2   The microscope.

The Industrial Revolution (1)

1 The more professional training, and the use of new scientific equipment, led to increased respect and a higher status.
2 They increased confidence in science and progress, and gave doctors better equipment and materials (for example, more powerful microscopes, better chemicals and drugs) which helped further discoveries and progress in medicine.

The Industrial Revolution (2)

1 It made vaccination compulsory. At that time, many still believed that governments should follow a laissez-faire policy.
2 It led to national rivalry – French and German doctors (for example, Pasteur and Koch) wanted to be the first to make the next breakthrough, and their governments provided money for research teams and facilities (for national prestige).

The drugs revolution (1)

For: Salvarsan was the first man-made 'magic bullet' which could kill microbes and so cure a disease. Before then, the methods used were vaccinations (Jenner) and anti-toxins (Behring). Eventually, others (sulphonamides) were discovered, and it could be said to have led to the discovery of penicillin.

Against: many doctors were reluctant to use it (it was painful, involved the injection of arsenic, might encourage promiscuity); and a second one was not discovered for another 20 years (1932).

The drugs revolution (2)

1 By chance, when he noticed a mould was growing on a Petri dish – and that no germs were growing near it.
2 Governments became prepared to grant money for research and production because of the great numbers of wounded soldiers (for example, the US government after Pearl Harbor – before then, Florey and Chain had been unable to persuade them to give help).

Medicine now

Similarities: both refer to potential problems with drugs. Source A mentions how some viruses/germs are now resistant to some antibiotics while Source B refers to 'new hazards' and 'risks'.

Differences: Source B also refers to 'greater benefits', while Source A mentions new diseases (for example, AIDS) and other factors (for example, 'ease of travel and communication') as being the causes of new health problems.

Women and medicine (1)

1 Because greater professionalism/specialist knowledge required secondary and university education and training, and women were excluded from most types of formal education by the Church.
2 There were few trained doctors – and they were expensive. So most people continued to rely on informal healers, such as housewife-physicians and 'wise women'.

Women in medicine (2)

Source A is useful as this is a cartoon that refers to the continuing exclusion of women from medicine, even in areas such as midwifery, which had often been seen as a natural role for women doctors and midwives. One reason for this was the invention of new instruments such as the obstetrics forceps, whose use required an advanced knowledge of human anatomy.

Public health to 1750

Source A shows lack of proper sewerage/sanitation in towns, and suggests that things are worse than before (and shows belief that 'contagious sickness', i.e. Black Death) might be caused by bad 'smells'/'filth' etc. This indicates a lack of proper medical understanding.

Source B also shows ignorance of the causes of the Black Death, hence ineffective responses.

Own knowledge: these show the decline in both knowledge/practical measures and government action since the fall of Rome. As towns grew in the Middle Ages, there were increased problems with water supplies and sewage disposal. At that time, medical knowledge/scientific developments were not able to show the links between dirt, germs and ill health.

Public health from 1750

1 Cholera.
2 Their discoveries showed how germs caused diseases.

Surgery (1)

His ideas were not accepted by most doctors who continued with traditional methods. His use of threads actually led to more infection, as there were still no antiseptics.

Surgery (2)

1 New weapons and methods of modern total warfare (for example, high explosives, petrol-driven machines) meant there were many more facial wounds and burns injuries.
2 The use of electricity and the invention of new machines, equipment and materials (X-rays, artificial kidney and heart-lung machines, electro-cardiographs, plastic joints, fibre optics, etc.) have allowed the development of new skills and specialisms, such as heart transplants and micro-surgery.

The American West, 1840–1895

The USA and the West

1 Thomas Jefferson.
2 Texas, Oregon and California.

The Plains Indians (1)

It mentions the importance of 'counting coup' against an enemy. This was even more important than killing him. It also stresses the idea of keeping casualties low, and the practice of scalping. However, the source doesn't say anything about white methods of warfare, and is only about the Cheyenne, who were just one of the many different nations of Plains Indians. But such methods were different, as whites tended to fight more large-scale battles which resulted in higher casualties – and scalping was also done by some whites.

The Plains Indians (2)

1 They provided almost everything the Plains Indians needed – food, shelter, clothing, tools, weapons and fuel.
2 To keep the tribes in harmony with nature and the spirits of the natural world – and particularly to protect the tribe.

Pioneers and wagon trains

The opening up of trails such as the Santa Fe and the Oregon Trails made it possible for a huge wave of settlers to move west to Oregon and California after 1840. Because the journey west was long and dangerous, the trails reduced the risks. There were many wanting to move because of the high price of land in the East, and the financial crisis of 1837. The US government, as part of 'Manifest Destiny' encouraged this and published maps of the trails. From less than 1000 people travelling in 1843, numbers grew to over 15000 in 1848, but this began to disrupt the lives of the Plains Indians.

The Gold Rush and the railways

1 1848.
2 The American Civil War.

Cattle and cowboys

The main problems were cattle stampedes; river crossings; blizzards; drought; Indian raids; conflicts with homesteaders; white rustlers or robbers (Jayhawks); boredom (the drives sometimes lasted four months).

Homesteaders

1 Buffalo chips.
2 Any two from: children/the house and housework/ growing vegetables/looking after smaller animals/ helping with heavier work at busy times.

Law and order

1 Any one from: lack of trustworthy law officers/ distance from Washington/slowness of decisions/quite easy for criminals to escape capture.
2 Areas with less than the 60000 inhabitants needed to become a state – these were ruled directly from Washington.

The struggle for the Great Plains

Probably not intended for publication as it is a report, so more likely to be truthful. The author, a US government Indian Agent, is also probably writing from first-hand observation – and the date (1853) is only two years after the treaty. He is also not trying to hide the problems (he refers to Indians being 'pinched with want' and 'crying with hunger'). However, this is only one man's view of one area – it might not be typical (though in fact it does describe the problems common on most reservations – often due to corrupt agents and poor soil and hunting).

The Plains Wars, 1860–1890

1 It wanted to exploit the gold in the Black Hills of Dakota which had been given to the Sioux as part of their reservation.
2 Sitting Bull and Crazy Horse.

Germany, 1918–1945

Changes in Germany

1 The army had kept secret recent defeats/no Allied troops had reached Germany.
2 They wanted Germany to become a workers' state, like Russia after the Bolshevik Revolution in November 1917.

Weimar Germany, 1919–1923

1 Germany had said it could not afford to pay its second reparations instalment, so France and Belgium went in to take coal and iron instead.
2 This was when the German currency collapsed – prices rose rapidly and money became worthless (even a stamp cost millions of marks).

The founding of the Nazi Party

The photograph shows the violent nature of the Putsch (men with weapons) and the role of the SA (two of the armed men are wearing swastika armbands), and the caption refers to Nazi Stormtroopers (the SA). Finally, the caption refers to the arrest of the mayor – Hitler and the Nazis had taken over a political meeting in a beer hall in Munich and had tried to get the political, police and military leaders to support their putsch. At first, they had agreed, but later changed their minds.

Germany before the Depression

1 After his failed attempt to overthrow the Weimar government in November 1923, he had been imprisoned, and the Nazi Party had been banned and had begun to break up. Also, by 1924, the economy had started to improve under Stresemann.

2 He relaunched the party in 1925, and gave himself greater control; special sections were set up to attract support from specific groups (for example, farmers, teachers, and the Hitler Youth for young people); and the SS was set up. He also began to reassure wealthy industrialists about his real intentions.

The Nazis come to power

1 The SPD, Centre Party and the DNVP.

2 It shows lots of parties had seats in the Reichstag – even quite small ones. This was a result of the system of proportional representation set up by the Weimar Constitution, which often led to frequent coalition governments. The constant changes made it difficult to cope with the serious political and economic problems of this period. The source also shows the increased support for extremist parties following the Wall Street Crash and the Depression after 1929.

The Nazi dictatorship

They used the laws of the Weimar Constitution to quickly establish emergency powers (the Enabling Law) after the Reichstag Fire – the Communists were banned and their leaders arrested (as Source A shows). Because of the lack of unity and co-operation on the left, the SPD did nothing at first. The Nazis then used their SA to intimidate opponents; trade unions were banned, and many trade unionists were put in concentration camps. Other parties were then persuaded to disband or merge with the Nazis. So in a matter of months, Hitler had turned Germany into a one-party state.

Nazi economic policy

1 Any two from: Jews, women and Communists were sacked and their jobs given to unemployed men/those in concentration camps did not count as unemployed/conscription was increased/the National Labour Service was expanded/public works provided jobs/the push for self-sufficiency and rearmament also provided new jobs.

2 He was opposed to the rearmament programme and Goring's Four-Year Plan, which undermined his attempts to improve the German economy.

The Nazi 'Volksgemeinschaft'

1 They were forced out of state and professional jobs/encouraged by loans and medals to be housewives and have large families/most of the equal rights gained under the Weimar Republic were removed/abortion became illegal and family planning advice was reduced/even their clothes, hairstyles and make-up were expected to conform to the Nazi 'ideal' of an Aryan woman.

2 Young people were seen as the future – if the Nazis could influence them with their propaganda, then their Nazi Reich would stand a good chance of surviving for 1000 years. It was also important that young men, in particular, were fit for war.

Outside the Nazi 'community'

The photograph shows Jewish women and children being loaded onto trains that would take them to the extermination camps and the Holocaust. One of the children is clearly wearing the yellow star of David, which the Nazis made all Jews wear.

At first, Jews in Germany – and then in the countries invaded by the German army – were discriminated against (for example, they were kicked out of jobs and schools, their shops were taken over, they were forced to live in ghettos). Then, in the Final Solution, about six million Jews were exterminated in the death camps. So, to this extent, the statement is correct.

However, the Nazis were also racist towards other groups, especially the Slavs and the Sinti and Roma people (gypsies), both of which suffered racial discrimination and then extermination. The numbers of other 'racially inferior' people murdered by SS 'Special Action' squads and in the extermination camps totalled about five million. So, overall, the statement is not correct – although more Jews were killed than any other group.

Opposition

Source A is useful as it gives details of some of the political groups (SPD and the Communist Party) that organised opposition to the Nazis. It also tells us some of the things they did – for example, writing anti-Nazi slogans – and even refers to sabotage and treason – the Communist Red Orchestra Group gave military secrets to the USSR before they were captured by the Gestapo. As it is from a history book written in 1994, the information should be accurate and reliable.

Source B is less useful, as it only shows a damaged room. However, the caption refers to the July Bomb Plot, 1944 – this is evidence of the opposition to Hitler and the Nazis from sections of the army elite. Apart from von Stauffenberg, who organised this unsuccessful attempt on Hitler's life, there was also the Beck-Goerdeler group.

However, neither of these sources say anything about opposition from young people (for example, the Eidelweiss Pirates or the White Rose Group) or from some religious groups. Finally, none of the sources give any indication of the numbers who resisted the Nazis.

Key terms

Medicine through time

Anaesthetic a drug to make a patient unconscious, and therefore unaware of pain during surgery

Antibody a defensive substance produced in the body to neutralise a foreign micro-organism or poison

Antibiotic a drug made from a living organism, such as fungi, which kills bacteria or prevents it growing

Antisepsis the use of antiseptics (first carbolic acid) to kill germs

Anti-toxin a substance, produced by the body to fight the poison/toxin introduced by a germ, which can be injected into another person to cure a disease

Apothecary someone (without formal medical training, at first) who sold drugs/medicine, usually from a shop

Asclepion a healing temple in Ancient Greece (and Rome), dedicated to Asclepios, the god of healing

Asepsis sterilising the air, clothing and doctors' tools in the operating room to remove the risk of germs

Barber-surgeons barbers who also performed minor surgery and dentistry – used mainly by the poor

Bleeding a treatment, based on the Ancient Greek Theory of the Four Humours, to draw off an imbalance/excess of blood (later called venesection)

Cauterise a method of treating amputated limbs or wounds by burning them with hot iron (cautery) or oil to prevent infection and seal the wound

Clinical observation the close observation and recording of a patient's symptoms, followed by appropriate treatment, stressed by Hippocrates and his followers (in part, developed from Ancient Egyptian medicine). It is the basis of modern scientific medicine

Embalming the practice of preserving a corpse from decay, sometimes called 'mummification', which was popular in Ancient Egypt

Inoculation an early method of protecting people from a disease, by infecting them with a milder form of the disease, in the hope of giving immunity (hence: immunisation)

Magic bullet a man-made chemical, designed to cure a disease by acting like an antibody, without harming the rest of the patient's body

Natural something which is physical, observable and of this world

Pilgrimage a journey to a shrine or holy place

Plague there are two main types: bubonic (with buboes or lumps), spread by flea bites; and pneumonic (respiratory), spread by coughing or sneezing

Plastic surgery specialised surgery to repair badly damaged skin or birth defects

Quacks doctors who sold useless pills, etc., often at fairs or markets, mostly to poor people – such medicine was known as 'quackery'

Regimen Ancient Greek belief that in order to be healthy, proper diet, sleep, exercise, etc. were important

Renaissance rebirth; marked the transition from medieval to early modern history beginning in the fourteenth century; a period when the arts and sciences flourished

Thalidomide a drug, withdrawn in 1961 because it was found to cause malformation in the fetus if taken during pregnancy

Theory of the Four Humours Ancient Greek medical belief that the body was made up of four substances, or humours. Any imbalance caused illness, so treatments were designed to restore balance

Trepanning the cutting of a hole in a live person's skull – also known as trephining

Vaccination a safer and more effective method of immunisation, based on controlled vaccines to give immunity to specific germs

Wise women local women who gave medical advice and help – used mainly by poor people

The American West 1840–1895

Buffalo chips dried buffalo dung used as fuel on the Great Plains, by both Native Americans and the early homesteaders

Cattle barons owners of large cattle ranches who formed powerful associations and took over smaller ranches in the 1880s

Coolies derogative name applied to immigrant Chinese railway workers

Counting coup the practice of Native American warriors of rushing towards an enemy and touching him with a coup stick (a pole about 8–10ft long) – considered more honourable than killing

Dugouts early homesteader dwellings hollowed out of hillsides (many places lacked trees for log cabins)

Elders older male members of a Native American band or tribe, who were part of a council that made decisions. They were helped by soldier societies (for example, the Dog Soldiers of the Cheyenne)

Federal Territories areas of the West which were not yet full states of the USA – the federal (central) government appointed marshals and judges to help maintain law and order

Ghost Dance a dance taken up by the Sioux Nation in 1890 – associated with Wovoka who said the dance would bring back all dead warriors and buffalo, and make the whites disappear. It was ended by the Massacre at Wounded Knee, November 1890

Great Plains the huge, often barren, grasslands (prairies) west of the Mississippi – in 1840, the Plains Indians and about 60 million buffalo lived there (whites called it the 'Great American Desert')

Great Plains Massacre the deliberate extermination of the buffalo in the 1870s by organised hunting (for leather), encouraged by the government, who saw it as a way of forcing the Plains Indians on to reservations. By 1875, less than one million buffalo were left; by 1890, there were only about 250

Great Spirit a name given by those Plains Indian Nations that believed in one supreme being/creator – other names included Father of Life, or Wakan Tanka (the Great God)

Homesteaders early pioneer settlers/farmers encouraged by US government acts and land grants in the 1860s to farm on the Great Plains – this began a large migration to the new Western Territories

Long Drive the journey made by cattle and cowboys from Texas to the cattle towns – it could last two months

Lynching the illegal hanging by unauthorised people (for example, vigilante groups) of someone suspected of a serious crime

Manifest Destiny the belief by whites that they had a God-given right to rule the whole of the USA, including (after 1840) the Great Plains where the Native Americans lived

Medicine men Native Americans believed by their tribe to have magical and/or healing powers – those with mainly religious roles were known as shamans

Mountain men early fur trappers who also helped open up the West by working out new trails (routes) and acting as scouts for the wagon trains of early pioneers

Nations the main groupings of Native Americans – each nation had its own language and culture, and was subdivided into tribes and bands

Native Americans all the Indians living in America before the arrival of the first white people – sometimes called (Red) Indians or American Indians

Nomadic a lifestyle based on hunting, requiring people to move frequently in order to follow the animals hunted (for example, buffalo on the Great Plains)

Permanent Indian Frontier the 'border' along the Mississippi, first agreed in 1830 between the US government and Native Americans. All land west was promised to the Indians – but this and later agreements were frequently broken by US governments (for example, the border moved further west to the 95th meridian)

Pioneers the very first white settlers to begin the move westwards

Range War a violent conflict between rich cattle barons and homesteaders – for example, the Lincoln County War and the Johnson County War

Reservations areas of land (often poor) 'granted' by US governments to Native Americans – they were supposed to stay on them and whites were meant to stay out

Rustlers gangs who stole cattle on the ranges and the Long Drives – for example, Jayhawkers

Scalping cutting off the skin and hair on the top of the head of a dead enemy. Plains Indians believed it prevented them having to meet their enemy in the afterlife – it also brought prestige/honour to the warrior. It was also practised by some whites

Sod houses another early type of homesteader dwelling – better than dugouts, they were made out of timber and turf bricks, with roofs made of sod and grass. Though cool in summer and warm in winter, they were impossible to keep clean, and they were damp and attracted insects

Trailblazers mountain men and fur trappers who surveyed/pioneered the first trails (routes) west – for example, the Oregon Trail, the California Trail

Transcontinental the spreading of the USA across the country, to link the Eastern/Atlantic territories with the new Western/Pacific territories – for example, by transcontinental railroads

Twister raging high wind/tornado common on the Great Plains

Vigilantes people who (often because of the lack of reliable law officers) formed vigilance committees, and punished suspected law breakers (for example, by hanging/lynching)

Wagon trains groups of pioneers travelling west together in wagons (pulled by oxen, mules or horses), led by a pilot (captain)

Germany 1919–1945

Anti-semitism racism against semitic (especially Jewish) people

Aryan a white person of non-Jewish descent

Beer Hall Putsch Hitler's failed attempt to seize power in 1923. Also known as the Munich Putsch or the National Revolution

Coalition a government made up of two or more parties

Concentration camps camps in Germany for the Nazis' political opponents – the camps' first victims were Communists and Social Democrats. Not to be confused with the later extermination/death camps in Eastern Europe, set up by the Nazis for the Final Solution

Enabling Act the law pushed through after the Reichstag Fire which allowed Hitler to issue decrees without needing the Reichstag's approval – supposed to be an emergency measure for just four years

Final Solution Nazi policy to wipe out the Jewish race in Europe

Freikorps right-wing ex-First World War veterans (often unemployed) who formed armed gangs. Used to suppress the Spartacist Revolution; many later joined the Nazi Stormtroopers

Führer means leader – used of Hitler especially after 1934 when he combined the roles of President, Chancellor and Commander-in-Chief of the armed forces

Gestapo the secret state police, first run by Goring, then, after 1936, by Himmler

Hitler Youth the various youth organisations (according to age and gender) set up by the Nazis to indoctrinate the young

Hyper-inflation vast increase in the cost of living due to the devaluation of the mark

July Plotters those involved with von Stauffenberg in the unsuccessful attempt (20 July 1944) to blow up Hitler

Kristallnacht Crystal Night, or Night of the Broken Glass, when thousands of Jewish businesses were destroyed

Länder the 18 local states/provinces of Weimar Germany

National Reich Church set up for Protestants by the Nazis in 1936, but many resisted

Night of the Long Knives purge of the SA (Brownshirts) by Hitler

Nuremberg Laws the anti-Jewish laws of 1935

Passive resistance resistance/opposition which tries to avoid violence – for example, strikes, boycotts, non-co-operation. Used by Germans in 1923 after the French invasion of the Ruhr

Putsch sudden attempt to remove a government by force

Reichstag German parliament

Reparations compensation/indemnity payments – imposed on Germany after the First World War (£6600 million)

SA Nazi Stormtroopers (Brownshirts) led by Rohm

SS Schutz-Staffel (Blackshirts) – elite bodyguard for Hitler which, under Himmler, grew in size and importance. Used to purge the SA in 1934

Sinti a group of people who, along with the Roma, are often referred to as gypsies

Slavs people of Eastern Europe speaking the Slavic language – according to Nazi racism, Slavs (like Jews) were inferior

Spartacists members of the Spartacist League, led by Karl Leibknecht and Rosa Luxemburg who, in 1919, tried to start a Socialist Revolution. Crushed by the Freikorps, many of the survivors went on to form the German Communist Party (KPD)

The 3 Ks Kinder, Kirche, Kuche (Children, Church, Cooking) – the Nazi view of a woman's role

War Guilt Clause article 231 of the Treaty of Versailles – Germany was forced to admit total responsibility for causing the First World War and to promise to pay reparations (compensation)

Weimar Republic Germany's political system from 1918–1933. Set up by the Weimar Constitution, it was Germany's first experience of real democracy

Last-minute learner

- These eight pages give you the most important facts across the whole subject in the smallest possible space.
- You can use these pages as a final check.
- You can also use them as you revise as a way to check your learning.
- You can cut them out for quick and easy reference.

Section 1: Medicine to AD500

Prehistoric medicine
- Prehistoric people were nomadic hunter-gatherers living in small groups.
- They had little understanding of causes or cures of illness. Instead, illness was explained by belief in the supernatural and evil spirits.
- Shamans (medicine men) and magic rituals played a big part in prehistoric medicine.
- Because of belief in evil spirits, one 'cure' that was used was the trephining (trepanning) of skulls.
- However, evidence suggests that prehistoric medicine also involved the use of natural or practical common-sense cures.
- Trephining actually forms a link in this dual approach to medicine – evidence shows that the bone healed over after the operation, showing the 'patient' survived. Such a procedure is now known to help in some cases of head injuries and epilepsy.
- They also used herbal medicines, ointments, natural dressings for wounds (for example, moss) and knew how to set bones and carry out amputations.
- But, as there is no written evidence, historians also have to rely on archaeology, ethno-archaeology and anthropology to try to understand prehistoric medicine.

Ancient Egyptian medicine
- The Ancient Egyptian civilisation along the fertile banks of the River Nile also had a dual approach to medicine.
- They believed evil spirits caused illness, and believed some gods (for example, Sekhmet, Thoth) helped bring about cures.
- Prayers by priests, and the use of charms and amulets, were believed to help prevent illness.
- However, the Ancient Egyptians also had a wide range of natural or practical cures based on herbal ointments and potions, and natural drugs and antiseptics. They also performed simple operations and stressed the importance of a healthy diet.
- Their invention of writing (hieroglyphics on papyrus) allowed symptoms and treatments (and their success or failure) to be recorded.

- This led to continuity, and allowed the training of doctors, who had to follow strict rules.
- Their practice of mummification led to improved knowledge of human anatomy (although they were not allowed to examine the organs removed). In addition, the insistence of priests on cleanliness led to improved hygiene.

Ancient Greek medicine
- Belief in gods and supernatural explanations of the causes and cures of illness continued in Ancient Greece. Particularly important was the cult surrounding Asclepios, the god of healing (and his daughters, Hygeia and Panacea).
- Asclepions (temples to Asclepios) were also used for treating the sick – usually done by priests who combined the use of ointments with prayers and rituals.
- However, some philosophers began to offer rational and natural explanations for the causes of illness.
- Particularly important was Hippocrates who based his work on earlier theories about the four elements, the need for balance and the importance of regimen.
- He stressed the importance of clinical observation of patients and symptoms, but he said little about treatment.
- His ideas were developed further by his followers in a collection of medical books known as the Hippocratic Corpus.
- Especially important was Aristotle who developed the Theory of the Four Humours, and methods to restore balance.
- Further medical progress resulted from the founding of Alexandria, in which a large library containing many medical books was established and, for a time, human dissection was allowed.
- Greek doctors and their ideas spread across the ancient civilisations around the Mediterranean.

Ancient Rome
- At first, after the Romans had conquered Ancient Greece, they rejected many of the Greek ideas about medicine.

- Later, an Asclepion was built in Rome and became a public hospital for the poor. Gradually, Greek doctors were allowed to practise, and they soon dominated medicine in the Roman empire.
- However, because there were few doctors, heads of households were supposed to treat their members – mainly using a mixture of common-sense practical cures and religious rituals.
- The Romans are particularly associated with practical achievements and developments in what is known as public health.
- This practical approach included the building of aqueducts, sewers, public baths and toilets, and the draining of swamps.
- Also, because of their desire for a strong army, attention was paid to treating ill or injured soldiers. This included clean drinking water, the safe disposal of sewage, hospitals for the wounded (valetudinaria), and special doctors and medical troops.
- Some of these were eventually extended to civilians.
- The most famous doctor in Ancient Rome was Galen, who developed the ideas of Hippocrates, and based his cures on the theories of balance and treatment by opposites.
- He wrote over 100 books, which drew together the ideas of all the doctors of the ancient world, to form a single system. This influenced medicine through the Middle Ages and into the Renaissance.
- But, because human dissection was not allowed (for religious reasons), Galen used dogs, pigs and apes – this led to some important mistakes about human anatomy.
- From about AD400, the Roman empire began to fall to northern tribes who destroyed books and libraries, so much of this medical knowledge was lost in Europe for a long time.

Section 2: Medicine, 500–1750

Islamic medicine

- Although the fall of Rome led to regression in medicine in Europe, much of the medical knowledge and books of the ancient civilisations were preserved in the East.
- Especially important in this was the new Islamic civilisation established in the Middle East.
- Although many Islamic doctors continued to believe that illness was caused by evil spirits, some based their work on the ideas of Hippocrates and Galen.
- Particularly important was Hunain ibn Ishaq (Johannitus) who became chief physician of Baghdad, the new capital of this Islamic empire.
- He travelled to Greece to collect medical texts, which he then translated into Arabic. This was in the ninth century, when much of this knowledge was still unknown in Europe.
- Islamic governments set up medical schools and, from 931, doctors had to pass exams to get a licence to practise.
- The main cities had public health services – piped water, public baths and hospitals (care of the sick was a duty in the Qur'an).
- Eventually, these ideas began to spread to Europe because of increased trade and the Christian Crusades.
- Also important were: Rhazes (al-Razi) who wrote the *al-Hawi* (*The Comprehensive Book*); and Ibn Sina (Avicenna) whose *Canon of Medicine*, based on Galen and his own observations, was later translated into Latin and became the main medical textbook in Europe until 1700.
- Arab alchemists also discovered new methods and techniques that helped prepare drugs for treating the sick.

Medieval medicine

- In Europe, after the fall of Rome, there was a regression in medicine. Many books and libraries were destroyed, and the public health systems of the Romans collapsed.
- Although the Christian Church gradually re-established itself, this did not help progress in medicine at first, as the Church believed in supernatural causes and cures of illness.
- As a result, there was much emphasis on prayers to God and the saints, and on pilgrimages.
- However, increased trade and the Crusades led to the medical knowledge and books of Islamic doctors reaching Europe – many of the works of Hippocrates and Galen were translated from Arabic into Latin.
- During the eleventh century, the Church came to accept the ideas of Hippocrates and Galen, but insisted these were the absolute truth (though not all of their works had yet been recovered). The Church also banned any human dissection.
- Many medieval doctors also saw astronomy and astrology as causing and/or curing diseases, and being useful for deciding diagnosis and treatment.
- Because doctors were few and expensive, most ordinary people relied on informal healers.
- Then, towards the end of the eleventh century, medicine became increasingly professional, and medical schools were established.
- From about 1300, the Church also began to allow some public dissection of human corpses in universities, and even accepted some revisions to Galen.
- However, acceptance of new ideas was slow – for much of the time, medical knowledge in Europe was behind that in the Islamic world.

- A particular problem in the Middle Ages, as trade grew and towns expanded, was public health.
- After the collapse of Rome, central governments did not provide public health facilities. Instead, it was left to the corporations of each town.
- The problems of unclean drinking water and sewage disposal led to many outbreaks of disease.
- However, the monasteries did maintain some continuity, especially as regards water supply, toilets and care of the sick in hospitals.
- In 1348, the Black Death hit England, and brought public health issues to a head.
- In all, about one-third of the population died, and it was worse in the towns. People had no idea about the disease's causes, or how to cure it.

Renaissance medicine

- Around 1450, a more scientific approach began to develop in Europe – this period became known as the Renaissance.
- In medicine, this led to the recovery of more texts by Hippocrates and Galen, but there was also a greater emphasis on observation and science.
- Printing helped spread new ideas, while the Reformation weakened the hold of the Church over education.
- Particularly important was Vesalius who discovered errors in Galen's anatomical work, and criticised the method of bleeding. But Vesalius had little to say about the causes or cures of illness, and so had little impact on treatment.
- Further progress was made in the seventeenth century – particularly important were Fabricius and his student, Harvey.
- Harvey proved that Galen was wrong about the heart and the circulation of blood, but this discovery failed to lead to any real changes in medical treatment.
- The Scientific Revolution led to a new interest in science and experimentation. One important invention was the microscope by van Leeuwenhoek in 1693. In the early eighteenth century, thermometers were invented, and different gases discovered.
- Further improvements in medical knowledge were made by Boerhaave and van Haller.
- Despite this, before 1750, most ordinary people had to rely on 'informal healers'. Supernatural and magical 'cures' still continued.

Section 3: Medicine from 1750 to the present

Medicine in the Industrial Revolution

- One effect of the Scientific Revolution was to increase respect for physicians and doctors, and to improve the training of surgeons.
- In the main, though, many old medical ideas continued in the first half of the eighteenth century.
- Also, despite the discoveries before 1750, doctors had little idea about the causes of disease. Knowledge of chemistry was limited, and microscopes were not very powerful.
- However, from about 1750, Britain underwent important changes that created an industrial society.
- At first, this had a bad effect on public health in the large, overcrowded and dirty industrial towns. Governments continued a laissez-faire attitude and did nothing to intervene.
- Eventually, though, as a result of improved technology, there were better aids and chemicals for medicine, such as more powerful microscopes, new drugs and new machines.
- An important discovery was made by Jenner, who published the results of his successful vaccinations against smallpox in 1798.
- Jenner could not explain why it worked, so there was much opposition at first to this method. Eventually, though, the government made vaccination compulsory in 1853.
- The next breakthrough came in 1857 when Pasteur discovered the link between germs and disease (although only in plants and animals).
- This idea was then taken up by Koch who, in the 1870s and 1880s (using newer technology), was able to link particular germs to particular diseases.
- Pasteur's team became the first to discover effective vaccines (against chicken cholera and then anthrax). In 1882, they discovered a vaccine against rabies.
- But the important breakthrough regarding human disease was made by von Behring, who used anti-toxins to cure a child with diphtheria in 1891. Other anti-toxins soon followed.

The drugs revolution

- In 1884, it was discovered that antibodies attacked specific germs. After 1900, Ehrlich (who had not had much success in extracting natural antibodies) began to look for synthetic chemical 'magic bullets' to cure disease.
- Using new dyes produced by the German chemical industry, he eventually made a breakthrough in 1909 when his team found a dye (Salvarsan 606) which attacked syphilis. It was first tried on a human in 1911.

Section 3: Medicine from 1750 to the present (continued)

- But it was not until 1932 that a second 'magic bullet' (prontosil) was discovered by Domagk. In 1935, he used it to cure blood poisoning.
- A French scientist identified the active ingredient as a sulphonamide. This led to a range of new drugs, based on sulphonamide, to combat several diseases (although several had serious side-effects).
- The next breakthrough was made by Fleming in 1928 when, by chance, he discovered penicillin – this killed germs without harmful side-effects. But he was unable to find a way to produce pure 'mould juice'.
- Then, in 1938, Florey and Chain developed a method based on freeze-drying, but they could only produce small amounts.
- However, once the USA became involved in the Second World War, Florey and Chain were given money and equipment to mass produce penicillin.
- This led to the development of a whole range of antibiotics that wiped out many diseases.

Medicine now

- The twentieth century saw the development of 'high-tech' surgery with many complex procedures, and great improvements in nursing. The discovery of DNA has led to the new science of genetics and genetic engineering.
- But there have also been problems – the side-effects of some drugs, the costs of providing new treatments, and also the question of ethics in some areas (for example, human embryo research and cloning).
- There have also been problems with some drugs companies bringing out drugs too early, before adequate research into side-effects, or dumping unsafe drugs on the poorer developing countries in Africa and Asia.
- Over-prescription of antibiotics has led to some germs becoming resistant – the 'super bugs'.
- During the twentieth century, Liberal and especially Labour governments passed acts to set up a welfare state. In 1948, Labour established the National Health Service.
- But problems over costs and staff shortages have led to problems, such as long waiting lists.
- This, and problems associated with high-tech medicine, have led many people to turn/return to alternative methods, including herbal medicine, acupuncture and even supernatural 'cures'.
- Although some of these methods are now available from the NHS in some areas, the BMA remains doubtful about their effectiveness.

Section 4: Themes in medicine

Women

- Before 1500, most people had to rely on informal healers. Many of these were women, who dealt with all aspects of medicine, as physicians, surgeons and midwives.
- In the civilisations of the ancient world, women were allowed to practise as doctors (especially as midwives). This was also true of the Islamic civilisation.
- At first, this was also true in medieval Europe but, as medicine became more professional and under the control of the Church, women were increasingly excluded.
- However, as most people could not afford trained doctors, women continued to act as informal healers (for example, housewife-physicians, 'wise women' and midwives).
- The decline in women doctors continued during the Renaissance. The invention of the obstetric forceps even led to women being excluded from their role as midwives (although their informal role continued).
- The first signs of a return of women to formal medicine came in nursing, as a result of the work of Florence Nightingale in the Crimean War.
- The Nightingale School of Nursing was established and others followed. In 1900, there were 64 000 trained nurses. After the establishment of entry qualifications in 1919, nursing became a respected medical profession.
- But there were still no women doctors. However, after 1850, attitudes began to change.
- Elizabeth Garrett tried to qualify as a doctor in Britain, but no university would allow it. Eventually, she qualified in Paris in 1870. But, in 1876, as a result of the efforts by those such as Sophia Jex-Blake, all medical qualifications were opened to women.
- The move to greater equality was helped by the two world wars, which led to an increased demand for doctors, and then by the establishment of the NHS. The Sex Discrimination Act, 1975, also helped create more opportunities, but women are still under-represented in top medical jobs.

Public health

- Public health developments in the ancient civilisations (Egypt, Greece and especially Rome) did not survive the fall of Rome.
- During the Middle Ages, governments were unwilling to provide public health facilities, and often lacked money or power to enforce such measures anyway.

- Corporations of individual towns rarely did anything, unless there was a serious outbreak of disease – the worst example being the Black Death (bubonic plague), which first hit Britain in 1348.
- Even after 1500, during the Renaissance, there was no real progress. In fact, the growth of trade and towns, and frequent wars, often made the situation even worse.
- As a result, epidemics and plagues continued to break out across Europe (for example, the Great Plague of London in 1665–1666).
- The main problem was that people did not understand the causes of such diseases.
- However, with the Industrial Revolution, public health reached a crisis, with the filthy and overcrowded conditions in the large industrial towns. The result was a range of infectious diseases, such as typhus and TB.
- Particularly important was the outbreak of a new disease in 1831 – cholera.
- This eventually persuaded the government to set up an enquiry under Edwin Chadwick. His Report came out in 1842 and, after another outbreak in 1847, led to the passing of the first Public Health Act in 1848 (although its measures were not compulsory).
- The work of Snow, and then the discoveries of Pasteur and Koch on germs, followed by another outbreak in 1865–1866, led to the establishment of a Royal Sanitary Commission in 1869, and a new Public Health Act in 1875 (this was more effective as it made action compulsory).
- Further revelations about the effects of squalor on health (the Booth and Rowntree reports, and the Boer War, 1899–1902) led to further reforms by the Liberal government, 1906–1918.
- Evacuation during the Second World War revealed problems still existed and led to the Beveridge Report (1942) and the establishment of the NHS by the Labour government in 1948.
- However, problems remain concerning the impact of chemicals and fertilisers on drinking water and the air.

Surgery

- For most of the 5000 years until 1750, surgery's three main problems were pain, infection and bleeding.
- Although there was some improvement in knowledge and techniques in the ancient world, the collapse of Rome led to regression in Europe. Even the advances made in the later Islamic civilisation had no impact on surgery in Europe.
- During the Middle Ages, surgery was often left to assistants or even untrained barber-surgeons.
- However, some discoveries were made by: Hugh and Theoderic of Lucca (wine as a mild antiseptic); de Chauliac (his work was based on Mondino's *Anatomy* of 1316); John of Arderne (early forms of anaesthetics).
- Generally, though, such new ideas had little impact, and were rejected by most doctors.
- Further progress (on treatment of wounds, amputations and bleeding) in the sixteenth century by Paré, who became the most famous Renaissance surgeon, was also largely ignored at the time. In fact, as there were no antiseptics, Paré's use of threads actually increased the risk of infection.
- The next important development was in relation to pain – with Davy identifying nitrous oxide (laughing gas) as a possible anaesthetic in 1799.
- More important was the discovery of ether (1842) and chloroform (1847), but these had side-effects, too.
- Another problem was that overcoming pain led to longer and more complex surgery, but the lack of antiseptics and blood transfusions led to increased death rates (the 'Black Period' of surgery, 1846–1870).
- A breakthrough came with the work of Semmelweiss (1847); especially important was Lister (1867) who, using Pasteur's germ theory, used carbolic acid to prevent infection.
- Though this led to a greatly reduced death rate, there was opposition to this method at first.
- Then, in 1887, Neuber and Bergmann in Germany moved on from antiseptic to aseptic methods, so ensuring that germs did not even enter wounds.
- However, bleeding continued to be a problem until 1901, when Landsteiner discovered different blood groups.
- Further discoveries during the First World War by Hustin allowed blood to be stored more easily.
- The terrible injuries suffered by soldiers and civilians in the two world wars led to the development of plastic surgery (Gillies and McIndoe) and then heart surgery (Harken).
- Further inventions (X-rays, electrocardiographs, artificial kidney, heart and lung machines, and fibre optics) have led to transplants and key-hole surgery.

The American West, 1840–1895

Before 1840

- After winning independence from Britain in 1783, the USA soon increased in size as a result of purchases, deals and wars.
- In 1803, it bought Louisiana from France – this was a huge area stretching west from the Mississippi River to the Rocky Mountains, and contained the Great Plains.
- In 1819, the USA bought Florida from Spain, giving it control of all land east of the Mississippi.
- In 1830, the Indian Removal Act said that all Indian tribes still in the East had to move west into what, in 1832, was declared to be 'Indian Territory'. In 1834, the Permanent Indian Frontier was fixed by the US government along the 95th meridian.
- However, the idea of 'Manifest Destiny' led many white Americans to want to settle the West, especially after the mid-1840s when the USA gained more new territory. From 1848, many whites wanted to create one huge USA stretching from the Atlantic to the Pacific.
- But the Great Plains, which lay between, were home to the Plains Indians. The five most important nations of these Native Americans were the Sioux, the Cheyenne, the Comanche, the Crow and the Apache.
- These nations, further sub-divided into tribes and bands, were mostly nomadic hunters, depending mainly on the buffalo.
- Their attitudes and beliefs were very different from those held by most whites, especially as regards land ownership and nature.
- They also had different ideas about religion and warfare – many believed in several spirits, and thought proving bravery ('counting coup') was more important than killing the enemy.
- Before 1840, there were no real problems, as the numbers of whites in the West were few. Most were 'mountain men' involved in the fur trade, whose activities did not disrupt the Plains Indians' traditional way of life.

Developments, 1840–1895

- During the 1830s, most of these fur hunters and trappers had come to work for two large companies and, by 1840, the fur trade was in decline.
- Some of these 'mountain men' then acted as scouts or guides for those wanting to move west. At first, this was the result of the 1837 financial crisis in the East, and the scarcity and high price of land there.
- Numbers wanting to go west increased when Oregon (1846) and California (1848) became part of the USA. So these guides 'blazed' trails west and then acted as scouts to the growing number of wagon trains.
- This was encouraged by the US government as part of Manifest Destiny. By 1848, 15 000 white settlers had gone west, despite the hardships and dangers.
- At first, the Plains Indians had traded with these settlers as they crossed Indian Territory on their way to Oregon or California. But tensions increased as the numbers grew and disrupted hunting. As a result, the US government sent troops to build forts to protect the settlers.
- The numbers wanting to go west increased even more because of the California Gold Rush, which began in 1848. The expanding population in the West, and the growth of towns there, led to calls for improved communications and transport.
- Eventually, it was decided to build a railroad to join East to West. The first one was completed in 1869. Others were built in the 1870s and 1880s.
- However, this greatly disrupted the buffalo herds and so led to even more conflict with the Plains Indians.
- The cattle industry, which began in Texas, took off after the end of the American Civil War in 1865. By then, the USA was undergoing an industrial revolution. This, and the growing population of settlers in the West, led to a huge demand for meat.
- So large numbers of cattle were taken on the 'Long Drive' north from Texas to the new rail towns.
- Later, cattle ranches were established on the 'open range' of the Great Plains in order to avoid the hardships of the Long Drive. This was increased when cold storage and refrigerator cars on trains made transport of meat even easier.
- Although the cattle boom was over by 1887, ranching on the Great Plains continued.
- Another important change in the 1860s, especially after the Civil War, was the number of people wanting to settle as farmers on the Great Plains.
- Despite previous agreements with the Indians, the US government passed several acts to encourage this, especially the Homesteads Act in 1862. During the 1870s, many of the early problems of these homesteaders were overcome, and the numbers therefore increased.
- This expansion in the West led to several law and order problems – in part because of the lack of sufficient and reliable law officers and, for US Territories, the distance from the capital.
- However, despite some problems with gunslingers, outlaw gangs and vigilantes, by the 1870s and 1880s the main problem was the conflict between cattle 'barons' and homesteaders over the 'open range'.
- By then, though, the biggest conflict in the West was the growing struggle for control of the Great Plains.

- The US government then decided to drop the 'one big reservation' policy. In 1851, the Treaty of Fort Laramie set up separate reservations for each tribe, but there were frequent problems of poor food and corrupt agents.
- By 1860, there had been many small conflicts, especially on the South and Central Plains. So, in 1861, the Treaty of Fort Lyon (Fort Wise), replaced the 1851 treaty.
- But this, too, was soon broken and a more serious conflict led to the Medicine Lodge Creek Treaty in 1867. By 1869, the Cheyenne had been forced to accept these new terms.
- The Great Plains Massacre of the buffalo in the 1870s led to the Red River War, 1874–1875. This ended in defeat for the Kiowa and the Comanche.
- Trouble in the North Plains grew after 1866, when the Bozeman Trail was started across Sioux hunting grounds, in breach of the 1851 treaty, after gold had been discovered in the remote North-West.
- Red Cloud's War, 1867–1868, resulted in the Fort Laramie Treaty, which stopped the Trail and gave the Sioux the whole of South Dakota.
- But then, in 1874, gold was discovered there. When the Sioux refused to sell their land, the War for the Black Hills began in 1875.
- Despite their victory at the Battle of the Little Bighorn in 1876, the Sioux were eventually forced to return to their reservations in 1877.
- Life on the reservations was made worse by the Dawes Act of 1887; dissatisfaction led to the Ghost Dance craze in 1890, but the Massacre at Wounded Knee in December effectively ended the Plains Wars.

Germany, 1918–1945

1918–1923

- By October 1918, the Allied naval blockade (on top of the harsh winter of 1916–1917, which destroyed the potato crop) was causing serious food and fuel shortages in Germany.
- In October, the Kiel mutiny led to revolution and the abdication of the Kaiser. The new provisional government signed an armistice in November 1918. The left-wing Spartacist Revolt was crushed by the army and the Freikorps.
- The Weimar Republic was set up in 1919, with a new democratic constitution and elections based on proportional representation. In 1920, the Nazi Party was formed. It set up a paramilitary group known as the Stormtroopers (SA).
- The terms of the Treaty of Versailles and the introduction of democracy led to much opposition from the conservative and nationalist right, including Kapp's Putsch, 1920.
- When Germany fell behind with reparation payments, the French occupied the Ruhr in 1923. This led to economic collapse and hyper-inflation. The Nazis' Beer Hall Putsch in Munich failed, and Hitler was imprisoned.

1924–1929

- The German economy recovered under Stresemann. Reparation payments were reduced by the Dawes (1924) and Young Plans (1929) negotiated with the USA. Germany also received loans to rebuild its economy.
- Germany signed the Locarno Treaty (1925), joined the League of Nations (1926), and signed the Kellogg-Briand Pact (1928).
- As a result, support for extremist political parties declined during these 'Golden Years'. After release from prison, Hitler began to reorganise the Nazi Party.
- In October 1929, Stresemann died. Then the Wall Street Crash in the USA led to the Great Depression. Loans from the USA stopped, and unemployment in Germany rose rapidly.

1930–1933

- By 1932, six million Germans were unemployed, and Nazi support increased. Hindenburg increasingly ruled by decree, as coalition governments were short-lived.
- Support for extreme parties grew – as Communist support increased, Hitler's Nazi Party became more attractive to many conservative and nationalist Germans, especially wealthy industrialists.
- Hitler reassured wealthy industrialists that the Nazis had no intention of implementing the 'socialist' parts of their programme, and donations to the Nazi Party increased. In July 1932, the Nazis became the largest party in the Reichstag.
- The Nazis lost seats in the November 1932 elections, while the Communists increased their share again. Von Papen persuaded Hindenburg to appoint Hitler as Chancellor on 30 January 1933.

1933–1939

- Hitler immediately called for new elections in March. But the Reichstag Fire, February 1933, led to the banning of the Communists. The Enabling Act was passed. By July 1933, Germany was a one-party state.
- Terror (SS and Gestapo) and propaganda (Goebbels) were used to prevent opposition.
- Trade unions and strikes were banned in 1933. Instead, workers had to join the Nazis' German Labour Front.

Germany (continued)

- Opposition from more militant Nazis (especially from SA leader Rohm, and his supporters, whose plans angered the army High Command) was ended by the Night of the Long Knives in June 1934.
- In August, when Hindenburg died, the army supported Hitler becoming Führer.
- The Nazis dealt with unemployment by public works schemes. At first, to reassure big business, Schacht became Minister of the Economy. His 'New Plan' tried to strengthen the economy and create self-sufficiency.
- But in 1936, Goring was ordered to get Germany ready for war. His Four-Year Plan clashed with the 'New Plan' so, in 1937, Schacht resigned.
- Women were pushed out of some jobs and encouraged to marry and have large families. The Nazis also tried to control young people through the Hitler Youth.

- The Nazis began their anti-semitic policies in 1933. A boycott of Jewish shops, and the expulsion of Jews from the civil service, were followed by the Nuremberg Laws of 1935. Violence was stepped up after the Night of Broken Glass in 1938.
- Despite the risks, some individuals and groups continued to oppose the Nazis. Particularly important were youth groups such as the White Rose Group and the Eidelweiss Pirates, the underground cells of the SPD and KPD, and those in the army such as the Beck-Goerdeler group.

1939–1945

- After 1939 and the start of the Second World War, Nazi policy towards the Jews became more extreme. In 1942, the 'Final Solution' began, under SS supervision.

Your notes

your notes